I0796089

DOUGLAS DC-8

A Legends of Flight Illustrated History

WOLFGANG BORGMANN

Schiffer
Military History
4880 Lower Valley Road
Atglen, PA 19310

Other Schiffer books by the author
Douglas DC-4, DC-6, and DC-7: A Legends of Flight Illustrated History, 978-0-7643-6648-2

S.E. 210 Caravelle: A Legends of Flight Illustrated History, 978-0-7643-6650-5

Douglas DC-9: A Legends of Flight Illustrated History, 978-0-7643-6484-6

Library of Congress Control Number: 2025939775

Designed by Alexa Harris
Type set in Minion/DIN/Axia
Translated from the German by David Johnston

ISBN: 978-0-7643-7078-6
ePub: 978-1-5073-0649-9

Printed in India
10 9 8 7 6 5 4 3 2 1

Published by Schiffer Publishing, Ltd.
4880 Lower Valley Road
Atglen, PA 19310
Phone: (610) 593-1777; Fax: (610) 593-2002
Email: Info@schifferbooks.com
Web: www.schifferbooks.com

For Dirk and Marcus

CONTENTS

CHAPTER 1
INTRODUCTION

With this Legends of Flight volume, the series now includes all the types from the Douglas and McDonnell Douglas aircraft families—from the DC-1 to the final MD-11 and MD-95 airliners.

As in my previous works, I will take you on an imaginary journey through time. This time mainly in the 1960s and 1970s, though the active history of the Douglas DC-8 continues with a few examples still in service up to the time these lines were written.

Alongside the Boeing 707/720, the Convair models 880/990, the de Havilland Comet 4, and the Vickers VC10, the DC-8 was one of the four-engine jet types that first came into service during the golden age of aviation.

Compared to the previous era of long-haul propeller-driven airliners with piston engines, they set new standards in terms of cruising speed and passenger comfort. While the de Havilland Comet 1 from 1952 to 1954 already gave an idea of what it meant to fly long haul with a jet, but failed due to the then-unknown limits of material science, a second chapter of the jet age between the continents began for the first time in 1958, with the Comet 4 and the Boeing 707. This time it was here to stay and laid the foundation for today's long-haul air travel with wide-body jets and also increasingly narrow-body aircraft—such as the Airbus A321XLR.

Welcome aboard on a flight through the fascinating history of the Douglas DC-8, the first jet of the legendary Douglas family of aircraft. *SAS*

The DC-8 was loved by its pilots. Its modern and ergonomically designed cockpit set the example for the following DC-9 jet. For decades, the DC-8 and DC-9 from Douglas were serious competitors for Boeing. *SAS*

On airport ramps all over the world, the DC-8 caused excitement among passengers and aircraft enthusiasts alike. Here at the SAS hub of Copenhagen-Kastrup. *SAS*

Regular maintenance of its DC-8-32s' JT4A-9 engines was part of the daily routine for Swissair. *ETH Zurich*

The DC-8 era was an irretrievable time when flying was an elitist, extremely expensive means of transportation for the lucky few. Thanks to a cartel run by the International Air Transport Association (IATA), global airline association, which set the fares for all airlines, the airlines could compete with one another only on the basis of outstanding service. And they did this in a way that is unimaginable today in the form of "pure luxury"!

The DC-8 was a part of my family for all my life. Not as an original, of course, but in the form of stories at the dinner table and personal, unforgettable flights. Since my father was employed by the important DC-8 operator Scandinavian Airlines System (SAS) from the 1950s to the 1990s, and his love of aviation was passed on to me, the Douglas jets operated by SAS aroused my enthusiasm at an early age. This applied not only to the DC-8, but also to the legendary DC-9 and DC-10, which were used alongside the elegant "eights" in SAS colors.

Born into the DC-8 era, I was lucky enough to be able to live out my passion for this type several times with flights on board an SAS and a Swissair DC-8, be it on a long-haul flight on an SAS DC-8-63 in 1978 from Zurich to Bridgetown, the capital of the Caribbean state of Barbados, or on a spotter trip on a Swissair DC-8-62 from my home airport of Stuttgart in southern Germany to the neighboring major airport of Zurich. Time and again, Swissair used this short flight of just thirty minutes for crew training for its long-haul crews. As a result, DC-8-62s and DC-10-30s with the Swiss cross were frequently operated on the short scheduled flights to and from Stuttgart.

The Super Sixties converted into DC-8-70s by Cammacorp represented the final stage in the development of the original DC-8 design from the 1950s. The DC-8-72 displays its elegant lines in this photo. *NASA*

Many fans of the DC-8 regard the Super Sixty models the DC-8-62 (in accompanying photo) and the DC-8-63, with their sleek, aerodynamically shaped engine nacelles, to be the most-beautiful versions of the type. *ETH Zurich*

A beautiful forward view of the DC-8 prototype during one of its early flights. *Boeing*

Left side

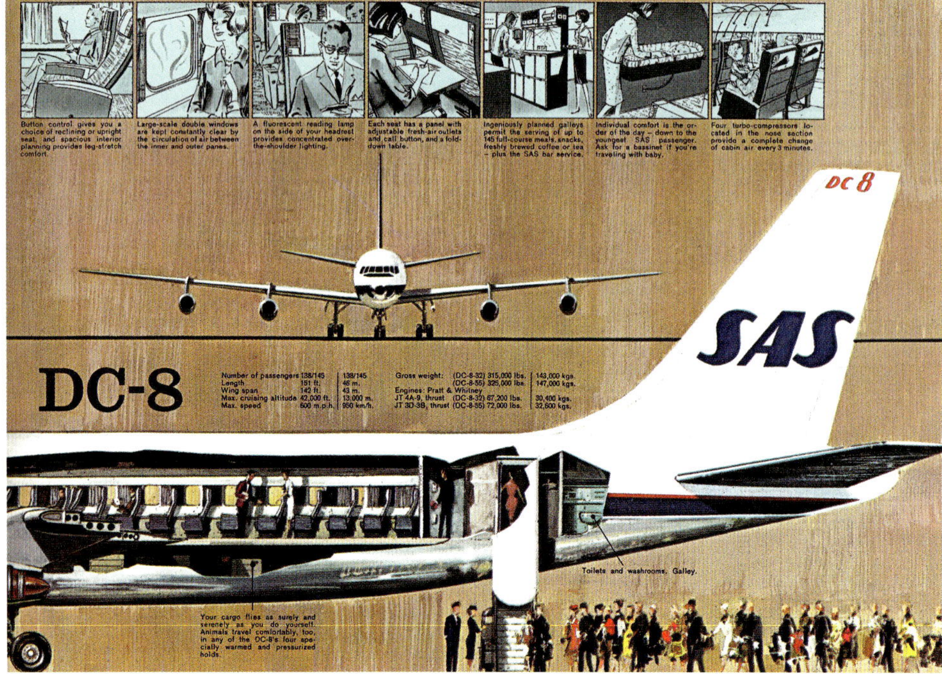

Right side of a complete picture

This cutaway drawing of an SAS DC-8-33 shows the layout of the passenger cabin and the cargo compartment located beneath it. *SAS / Wolfgang Borgmann collection*

The SAS DC-8-62 LN-MOW Roald Viking in its final SAS livery. The photo was taken at Copenhagen-Kastrup on September 22, 1984. *Dirk Grothe*

My last DC-8 flight took place in 1986. At a time when most of the DC-8s had already been sold off by the major airlines and replaced by more-modern types, SAS continued to operate its popular Douglas four-engined airliners. I flew as a passenger on the DC-8-62 Yorund Viking from Copenhagen to Chicago O'Hare. It was being used as a replacement for an unserviceable DC-10-30 and gave me an unforgettable "farewell" to this aircraft type.

With fewer seats than the wide-body jet, it was hopelessly overbooked and left many disappointed passengers in the Danish capital, whom SAS rebooked onto other flights. I, on the other hand, was lucky enough to get a seat in the last row of the jet. What others would see as a "punishment" was the greatest stroke of luck for me. It was the best place to enjoy the fabulous

BRIEFING FROM THE CAPTAIN
with elapsed times from departure

FLIGHT No. 便名 941 — DATE 日付 8/8 — NAME OF AIRCRAFT 機名 YORUND VIKING
PILOT IN COMMAND 当機の機長 B. SANDBERG — DESTINATION 行先 CHICAGO
MAÎTRE DE CABINE/PURSER 主任客室乗務員 K. EDBERG — DEPARTURE 出発 LOCAL TIME 現地時刻 1215 GMT 標準時 1015
TYPE OF AIRCRAFT 機種 DC8 — REGISTRATION 登録名 SE DBG — FLYING TIME 飛行時間 8:40
ESTIM. TIME OF ARRIVAL 到着予定時刻 LOCAL TIME 現地時刻 1355 GMT 標準時 1855
OUTSIDE TEMPERATURE 外気温 °C −20 −30 −40 −50 −60 −70 °C; °F −20 −40 −60 −80 −100 °F
ALTITUDE 高度 METERS メーター 9000 10000 11000 12000 METERS; FEET フィート 31000 35000 39000 FEET
SPEED OVER GROUND 対地速度
NAUTICAL MILES/HOUR 海里／時 400 500 600 700 KT/H
STATUTE MILES/HOUR マイル／時 500 600 700 800 MPH
KILOMETERS/HOUR キロ／時 800 1000 1200 KMH
SPEED THROUGH THE AIR 対気速度 — MACH マッハ 0.80
MACH 1.0=SPEED OF SOUND
WEATHER REPORTED AT NEXT LANDING つぎの到着地の天候
FAIR OVERCAST RAIN SNOW WINDY LIGHT/DARK
SAS 3426 b
ESSELTE MAP SERVICE, STOCKHOLM, SWEDEN 1984

This small slip of paper is among the treasures of this book's author. This "briefing from the captain" was passed through the cabin from one row of seats to another during SAS flight SK 941 from Copenhagen to Chicago on DC-8-62 SE-DMU. The sparse information that can be read on it was the only opportunity the economy-class passengers had to learn something about the progress of their flight prior to the introduction of the now-so-popular in-seat video screens. In first class, the purser went through the cabin with an inflatable globe on which the route of flight had been painted. It was definitely a different time! *Author's collection*

The author took this photo at the gate in Copenhagen prior to takeoff by flight SK941. *Author's collection*

First-class service on board an SAS DC-8-33. The Scandinavians were famous for their outstanding service during the "golden age of air travel." SAS

Loading an SAS DC-8-55RF at Copenhagen airport. The airline offered good service not only to its passengers but also to those in the freight business. SAS

sound of the four Pratt & Whitney JT3Ds, which would send shivers down the spine of any airplane fan. The "tamed" DC-8s, which Cammacorp and McDonnell Douglas retrofitted with quieter and more-economical CFM56 engines, were no comparison in terms of sound or appearance. This was surely a benefit to those living near airports and the environment, but a loss for all DC-8 fans!

The DC-8 was an impressive aircraft in every respect. The type's development potential was enormous, and at the time it entered service, the DC-8-63 was the largest aircraft in the world in terms of passenger seats and remained so until the Boeing 747 jumbo jet appeared. Numerous technical innovations gave it not only its typical "smile," but also outstanding passenger comfort and economy.

A DC-8-62 in its element. The contemporary SAS livery was supposed to be reminiscent of the Viking longships with which the early Scandinavians established new trade routes and settled new continents, including Iceland, Greenland, and North America.

With this photo of a friendly SAS crew posing in front of the DC-8-33 SE-DBA Rurik Viking, I wish all readers much pleasure in reading this book about the DC-8, Douglas's great four-engine jet airliner. *SAS*

This image of the distinctive engine nacelles of a DC-8-33 adorned the cover of an SAS brochure concerning the airline's fleet at the beginning of the 1960s.
SAS / author's collection

From today's perspective, the cabins of the first DC-8 models may seem somewhat antiquated. Curtains instead of today's familiar sun shades provided protection from the sunlight. This was a tribute to the piston-engined DC-7, which preceded it, from which Douglas adopted numerous ideas for the cabin design. The window spacing also hearkens back to the previous era of air travel, when entire aircraft were equipped exclusively with first-class seating. In the DC-8, too, those premium passengers initially flew in exclusive lounges above the clouds, where almost every wish was fulfilled. Only the Super Sixty models were optimized for the emerging mass air traffic of the late 1960s, their range and engine performance massively increased—and their cabins modernized. However, the DC-8 not only was intended for passenger air traffic but was also available as a pure freighter or as a combi aircraft from its early models. Its outstanding design is one of the reasons why a DC-8-72 freighter is still in service today with the humanitarian-aid organization Samaritan's Purse, long after the last of the competing passenger models were retired.

Welcome aboard for this fascinating journey back to a bygone era of air travel.

Wolfgang Borgmann
Bielefeld, autumn 2024

CHAPTER 2
HOW IT ALL BEGAN

THE DILEMMA: TURBOPROP OR PURE JET?

Company patriarch Donald Wills Douglas Sr. was in no hurry to bring his aircraft company, founded in 1920, into the jet age. In contrast to Boeing, the Douglas Aircraft Company had a considerable order backlog of 275 DC-6 and DC-7 propeller airliners when the British de Havilland Comet 1, the world's first production passenger jet, entered scheduled service on the other side of the Atlantic in 1952. Donald Douglas was also unsure as to whether the airlines would be prepared to replace their propeller-driven fleets, whose value had not yet depreciated, with faster jets just a few years after making a global investment of around 1.5 billion US dollars in new propeller-driven aircraft. After all, their aircraft would lose a lot of value as a result, and the airlines would be forced to accept considerable losses.

Douglas was the world leader in four-engine propeller-driven airliners. They were flown by airlines and transported heads of state—such as this American VC-118. *US Air Force*

C. R. Smith, president of Douglas's major customer American Airlines, was particularly skeptical of the new jet engine. He therefore urged Douglas to develop the DC-7 airliner, powered by Curtiss-Wright 3350 piston engines, to outperform the even-slower Lockheed L-1049 Super Constellation operated by its rival Trans World Airlines.

The DC-7 project was launched in 1951, while preparations for the jet age were in full swing in Great Britain and Canada and Boeing was already working on plans for its first civil jet airliner.

Although he had invested large sums in the new, old-technology DC-7, Donald Douglas wanted to keep at least one foot in the door of the emerging jet airline industry. In June 1952, therefore, he set up a small project office in Santa Monica, California, whose task was to prepare studies on a possible jetliner for the company. For Douglas, nothing less than the existence of the company was at stake, which had already fallen behind Boeing in this early planning phase.

No matter whom the Douglas engineers consulted, opinions on the right size for the project, now called the DC-8, differed widely. Pan American, in particular, pushed

Pan American originally planned to purchase neither the Boeing 707 or the Douglas DC-8. Had the de Havilland Comet program not been halted because of two crashes caused by material fatigue in 1954, Pan Am would have entered the jet age with the Comet 3s it had ordered. *Author's collection*

Pan Am president Jan Trippe initially preferred the Douglas DC-8, and his airline ordered twenty-five examples in 1955. Not until Boeing announced a wider fuselage for its 707 were the cards held by the two competing four-engine jet airliners reshuffled. *Marcus Kolskog collection*

for a jet with dimensions comparable to those of the Boeing 367-80 Dash 80 prototype jet aircraft, officially announced in April 1952. Other airlines, however, expressed a preference for a smaller jet with less seating capacity.

The plans conceived by Boeing and Douglas were made possible by the development of the Pratt & Whitney JT3 engine, which was derived from the J57, used to power military aircraft. Both Boeing and Douglas had already had good experience with the J57 in their own military jets and therefore counted on the reliability of the civil JT3 for the first versions of their four-engine passenger aircraft.

While the de Havilland Comet was withdrawn from service in April 1954 as the result of material fatigue and after a spectacular series of crashes, Boeing launched its 367-80 Dash 80 just three months after the British type was grounded. From it later emerged the Boeing 707 and the military KC-135. Douglas, on the other hand, having fallen behind due to the initial hesitation on the part of the company patriarch, had little more to offer at that time than initial designs and a wooden, albeit full-size, model of its prosed jet airliner's fuselage.

Official rollout of the DC-8 Ship One on April 9, 1958. *Boeing*

Close-up of Ship One taken during its rollout—in the background is one of the first production aircraft. *Boeing*

On May 30, 1958, the DC-8-11 Ship One, with the registration N8008D, took off on its maiden flight. *Boeing*

The final-assembly line at Long Beach. It was where all 556 Douglas DC-8s produced were built. *Boeing*

THE SETBACK

Douglas did not have the financial means to invest in a prototype jet aircraft comparable to the Boeing Dash-80 from its archrival from Seattle. Thus, there was all the more reason for the managers in Santa Monica to hope for a tender from the US military for a tanker aircraft in the DC-8 category. If the company's aircraft had been accepted, this would have offset some of the enormous development costs and thus secured the existence of the entire company. The shock was therefore all the greater in February 1955, when Boeing was awarded an exclusive contract by the US Department of Defense to supply twenty-one KC-135 tankers. While Boeing was able to cross-finance not only the KC-135 with this order, but also its Dash-80 test bed and the development of the 707 civil airliner, Douglas had to bear the entire cost of the DC-8 program itself. However, if the company wanted to continue to play an active role in civil aircraft construction, there was no alternative to continuing the DC-8 project.

PARALLELS WITH THE PRESENT DAY

The discussion at the time about sticking with traditional propulsion systems—or adopting turboprop or pure jet engines—is somewhat reminiscent of the climate-neutral propulsion concepts of the future that were being hotly debated at the time this book was written. All around the world, work is being carried out on new, "green" propulsion systems and concepts for the passenger aircraft of the next decade and beyond. Not only at national research institutions, such as the US's National Aeronautics and Space Administration (NASA) or the German Aerospace Center (DLR), its German partner, but also by the aircraft manufacturers Airbus, ATR, Boeing, and Embraer, as well as various engine manufacturers.

The driving forces behind this are the political requirement and public pressure to fly climate-neutrally by the middle of the twenty-first century. Various "disruptive" concepts are being investigated in order to achieve this lofty goal. In principle, engine and aircraft manufacturers have three options. Either they depend on climate-neutral

United Airlines and Delta Air Lines were the first customers to purchase the DC-8. United received its first example, Ship Eight, a DC-8-11 with the registration N8004U, in a ceremony on June 3, 1959. Aircraft N8028U, depicted on a United Airlines postcard, was Ship Three and flew for the first time on December 22, 1958. It was built as a DC-8-11; however, before it was delivered, it was modified to DC-8-12 standard. United received the aircraft on November 5, 1961, and in April 1965 converted it once again, this time into a DC-8-21. Ship 3 was scrapped in May 1983. *Marcus Kolskog collection*

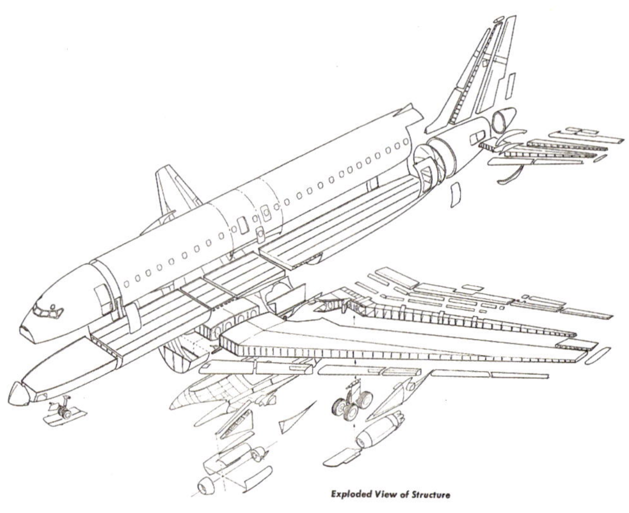

This 1959 drawing published by Douglas shows the internal structure of the DC-8. *Marcus Kolskog collection*

The cockpit of NASA's DC-8-72. *Dirk Grothe*

sustainable aviation fuel (SAF), or on "green" hydrogen, or they develop aircraft with battery-powered electric motors. Hybrid drive concepts with a combination of several alternatives are also conceivable—depending on the different energy requirements for each flight phase.

While researchers agree that SAF is the only fuel that can be considered for long-haul and wide-body jets, there has been movement in the design of new short- and medium-haul aircraft or small regional aircraft. The cards will soon be reshuffled here—and, as in the case of the Douglas DC-8 at the end of the 1950s, it remains exciting to see which ideas will prevail.

A GREAT SUCCESS

Douglas initially offered interested parties a DC-8A Domestic version for continental routes within the USA, for earliest delivery in 1956, and a DC-8B Overwater version from 1958—for international routes between the continents.

On October 13, 1955, Pan American president Juan T. Trippe announced an order for twenty-five DC-8s in the overwater version with advanced Pratt & Whitney JT4 engines. At the same time, he ordered just twenty Boeing 707-120s, which at that time were still offered with the narrower passenger cabin of the Dash-80 and KC-135. It could therefore be equipped only with five-abreast seating instead of the six-abreast seating of the DC-8. The future seemed particularly bright for Douglas after Trippe announced its intention to order more DC-8s instead of Boeing 707s.

Just twelve days after Pan Am, United Air Lines placed an order for thirty DC-8s, followed by the Dutch airline KLM as the first overseas customer. By the end of 1955, Douglas's order books had filled up with further orders from such prominent customers as Eastern Air Lines (twenty-six), National Airlines (six), Japan Air Lines (four), and Scandinavian Airlines (seven). The type's greater cabin width was a decisive criterion not only for Pan Am in favor of the DC-8. United Air Lines also favored the Douglas jet for this reason. However, the cards were reshuffled between Boeing and Douglas, at the latest when American Airlines was able to convince Boeing management to widen the fuselage of its 707 four-engine jet to enable six-abreast seating. The best argument in favor of this was an order for thirty Boeing 707s from American on November 8, 1955.

Development of the DC-8 took longer than Douglas had originally planned. In June 1956, the company announced the construction of a new final-assembly facility in Long Beach, California, specifically for the DC-8. The first aircraft parts were produced starting in September 1956, and, in addition to the production hall, Douglas built a huge water tank for material fatigue tests that could hold an entire DC-8 fuselage. After the fatal crashes of at least two de Havilland Comet 1s due to material fatigue, Douglas had fitted the DC-8 with small titanium crack stoppers on the fuselage frames as well as on all recesses such as doors, service hatches, and windows. After 113,000 simulated flights in the water tank, the first cracks appeared on an aluminum window frame. However, the stoppers did their job as planned and stopped the cracks from spreading with a large safety margin. By the time of the DC-8's maiden flight, the engineers had simulated 120,000 flights with the pressurized cabin activated and ended the program after a further 20,000 uneventful takeoffs and landings. The DC-8 had successfully proven its reliability.

FAMILY OF AIRCRAFT

The first example of the new Douglas type, dubbed Ship One, took to the skies for the first time on May 30, 1958. Following an extensive test flight program and certification by the US's Federal Aviation Administration (FAA) on August 31, 1959, launch customers United Air Lines and Delta Air Lines simultaneously put their previously delivered DC-8-11s into scheduled service beginning on September 18, 1959. This domestic version was followed by the DC-8-20, -30, -40, and -50 series, all variants with identical fuselage lengths but different power plants and ranges.

The DC-8 Super Sixty models, the DC-8-61, -62, and -63, represented the first major evolutionary step, offering stretched fuselages. The 62 and 63 series also featured Pratt & Whitney JT3D turbofan engines housed in slim engine nacelles. They also had aerodynamically redesigned wings and a much-greater range—the DC-8-62 had a range of around 10,000 km (6,214 mi.)!

The fuselage of the first DC-8-61 is moved to final assembly in the final-assembly line at Long Beach. *Boeing*

A short time later, the completed aircraft is seen in front of the final-assembly hangar. *Boeing*

Engine instruments of a Swissair DC-8-62. *ETH Zurich*

The Scandinavian airline SAS not only was the driving force behind development of the DC-8-62, the details of which were defined in a Stockholm hotel room by SAS and Douglas representatives, but also placed the first order for four Series 62 aircraft on April 4, 1965. As a pioneer of polar air transport, SAS was looking for a jetliner that could cover the distance between Scandinavia and the US West Coast nonstop, a task for which Douglas had customized its DC-8-62.

As well as SAS, many other European airlines were among the major customers for the DC-8, which was popular with both passengers and crews, including Alitalia, Finnair, Iberia, KLM, Swissair, and UTA. For many years the DC-8 was also operated by European charter airlines such as Air Spain, Atlantis, Balair, Sterling, and Südflug. And in August 1965, Lufthansa even leased the DC-8 prototype, now configured as a DC-8-55, for use on charter flights to North America.

A DC-8-72, converted from a DC-8-62 by Cammacorp, in flight. *SAS*

In North America the DC-8 was flown by many of the leading airlines, including Air Canada, Braniff, Canadian Pacific, Capitol, Delta, Eastern, Flying Tiger, United, Northwest, Seaboard World, Transamerica, World Airways, and the large express services UPS and TNT (these and other DC-8 operators around the globe can be found in chapter 6).

After it became apparent in the 1970s that stricter noise regulations would be coming into force, particularly in the United States, various North American airlines approached Douglas with a request to offer quieter engine options for their DC-8s that had been in service for many years. Pratt & Whitney offered its new JT8D-209 engine, while Cammacorp, founded by retired Douglas managers, offered the much-quieter and more fuel-efficient CFM-56-1 with which to convert DC-8 versions -61, -62, and -63. After United Air Lines and Flying Tiger Lines opted for the Cammacorp concept, further orders quickly followed, including from Delta Air Lines and Cargolux. One of the early operators of the DC-8-73 was the Lufthansa cargo subsidiary German Cargo, which contributed its five aircraft to Lufthansa Cargo AG, which was founded in 1994. One of them was temporarily equipped with a passenger cabin in 1985–86 and leased to Condor for its charter flights to North America.

In 1981, the US's FAA granted certification to the models now known as the DC-8-71, -72, and -73.

Maiden flight by Ship One on May 30, 1958, and the official handover ceremony for the last DC-8 to be built. The DC-8-63 with the registration SE-DBL was handed over to SAS on May 12, 1972. *Boeing/SAS*

DOUGLAS: LONG NUMBER ONE IN AIRCRAFT CONSTRUCTION

The Douglas factory in Long Beach, California. *Boeing*

When the DC-8 first took to the air in 1958, Douglas was the undisputed world leader in civil aircraft construction. Neither Boeing nor Lockheed could even come close to holding a candle to Douglas.

This unique success story, which lasted at least until the beginning of the jet age, was down to one man: Jack Frye. He was president of Transcontinental and Western Airlines (TWA), which laid the foundations for an unparalleled family of aircraft when it ordered the DC-1.

After the prototype made its successful maiden flight on July 1, 1933, the DC-1 received its type certificate just four months later. Jack Frye was enthusiastic about its great potential and was the first to order the larger DC-2, with a longer and wider fuselage. The next evolutionary step in the DC family was the result of a request from American Airlines president C. R. Smith. He planned to use an aircraft with fourteen double-decker beds on nightly transcontinental routes across the United States. The fuselage of the DC-2 was widened, the cabin ceiling raised, the wingspan increased, and a new tail designed. The DC-3, initially called the Douglas Sleeper Transport (DST), was born. On December 17, 1935, the prototype of this model took off on its maiden flight. With 455 civil versions sold and almost 20,000 examples of military variants produced, it is among the most built aircraft in the world.

The first four-engine airliner produced by Douglas was the brainchild of William A. "Pat" Patterson, president of United Air Lines, who approached Donald Douglas with an idea and 300,000 US dollars as a lure. Patterson

The water injection used to boost the power produced by the engines of early jets produced huge clouds of smoke. *Boeing*

was enthusiastic about the twin-engine Douglas products but was looking for production of an even-larger, four-engine airliner. Donald Douglas agreed to build the DC-4E Experimental, which could carry thirty passengers on night flights or forty-two passengers during the day with a level of comfort that far exceeded that on board the Douglas Sleeper Transport. A striking feature of the DC-4E was its triple tail, not unlike that of the Lockheed Constellation. As promising as the performance data for the DC-4E were, the airlines were reluctant to place orders with war approaching in Europe. Douglas had certainly developed a good aircraft, but one that was too large for a shrinking market. Even before the United States was drawn into the chaos of war, Donald Douglas decided to reduce the dimensions of a DC-4 production aircraft. And so, in Santa Monica, California, production work began on an initial batch of twenty-four DC-4As destined for American Airlines and United Air Lines.

Douglas had less luck with its DC-5: just thirteen of these twin-engine shoulder-wing aircraft, a development based on the Douglas A-20 Boston/Havoc bomber, left the final-assembly line at the Douglas plant in El Segundo.

In September 1938, Douglas began building the prototype, which took off on its maiden flight on February 12, 1939. In contrast to the previously developed aircraft types, the DC-5 was not created at the request of a customer, but because it was technically possible to further develop the A-20 into an airliner. However, with a seating capacity almost identical to that of the DC-3, the DC-5

View from the cabin window of a DC-8-11 of two of its four Pratt & Whitney JT4A power plants. *Boeing*

Swissair passengers were able to enjoy this view of their DC-8-32's four Pratt & Whitney JT4A engines. *ETH Zurich*

This view of the four power plants of the Super Sixty DC-8-63 will also probably never be seen again. *SAS*

Compared to the engine variants from the 1950s and 1960s, the CFM56 turbofan engines of the NASA DC-8-72 are real giants. *NASA*

offered no significant technical or operational improvements over its sister aircraft. As a result, there was no incentive for airlines to acquire this type. Ironically, it was Boeing founder and company owner William Edward Boeing who purchased the first completed DC-5 as a personal transport. The first customer for the production aircraft was the US Navy, which purchased three DC-5s, with the designation R3D-1, toward the end of 1939. Four further aircraft went to the US Marine Corps as the R3D-2. The only airline customer was the Dutch company KLM, which transferred the five aircraft it had ordered to KNILM, then based in the Dutch East Indies—now Indonesia—in 1940 due to the outbreak of the First World War in Europe.

With the DC-6 Cloudmaster, Douglas Aircraft Co. succeeded in building on the civil success of its legendary DC-3. Douglas sold 175 examples of the DC-6 and 286 of the more powerful DC-6B. On March 28, 1947, American Airlines and United Air Lines took delivery of their first aircraft in Santa Monica, California.

The Douglas DC-7C stood at the end of a long evolutionary chain of successful propeller-driven airliners from this manufacturer. The impetus for the development of the DC-7 again came from the president of American Airlines, C. R. Smith. He had already convinced Douglas to build the DC-3 in 1934, thus laying the foundations for the success story of the aircraft manufacturer based in Santa Monica, California. Smith now demanded a further development of the DC-6B, and the resulting Douglas aircraft took flight for the first time on May 18, 1953, in the form of the DC-7. On November 4, 1953, an aircraft of this type was used for the first time by American Airlines. The DC-7 also made nonstop flights between the American East and West Coasts possible.

Final assembly of the first DC-8-63. *Boeing*

Eastern Airlines initiated the DC-7B, which took to the skies for the first time on April 21, 1955, and had a range around 900 km (560 mi.) greater than that of the DC-7. It was followed by the ultimate DC-7C Seven Seas long-haul version. Launch customer Pan Am put the first aircraft of this type into service on April 18, 1956.

THE END OF INDEPENDENCE

For decades, Donald Douglas Sr. was regarded as the cornerstone of the American aviation industry. He successfully guided his company through the recession of 1939, continued to expand it during the war, and, as mentioned, was the undisputed market leader in the production of passenger aircraft even after the Second World War.

Donald Douglas Sr. was a company patriarch of the old school, who preferred to take the fate of his global corporation into his own hands by telephone rather than delegating tasks to his employees. His son Donald Douglas Jr. took over as CEO in 1957, and his aggressive management style led to an exodus of many talented employees from the company's management staff. After Douglas Jr. and his father, who remained chairman of the board and thus continued to hold a leadership role in the company, were only reluctantly able to decide to launch the company into the jet age, Boeing had built up a two-year lead with its 707, which had an impact on the initially sluggish sales figures for the Douglas DC-8.

Plagued by heavy losses from the DC-8, the company was saved from premature demise in the early 1960s only by its profitable missile and space division. Things went better for Douglas with the DC-9, which Boeing initially had no suitable model to counter. It was not until a few years later that the Boeing 737 was launched. Riding this wave of success, Douglas expanded DC-9 production capacity to such an extent that the DC-9, which was initially sold below production cost to stimulate demand, turned into a loss-making business. According to historical sources, Douglas lost around 1.25 million US dollars on each of the first twenty aircraft produced! Instead of making a good profit on its bestseller and building up a financial cushion for future projects on the horizon, such as the DC-10, Douglas slipped deep into the red over the course of 1966.

The situation was so dramatic that the company urgently needed an external financial injection to survive. In their search for the saving straw, father and son Douglas initially looked for financial investors and held talks with the

Rockefeller family and the eccentric aviation tycoon Howard Hughes, among others. These efforts were not the only ones to fail, however, leaving a merger with a financially healthier company as the only way forward. Some of the top companies in the American aviation industry, including North American and General Dynamics, initially showed interest, but in the end only McDonnell remained as a potential merger candidate. After James Smith McDonnell had already gotten the lowdown in January 1967 and acquired 300,000 Douglas shares on the stock exchange, which were offset by only 9,000 company shares held by father and son Douglas, the Douglas board of directors declared its willingness to merge with McDonnell on January 13, 1967.

On April 27, 1967, the new McDonnell Douglas Aircraft Company was launched with the independently operating divisions McDonnell Aircraft Company, Douglas Aircraft Company, and McDonnell Douglas Astronautics Company. The company headquarters were established at the former McDonnell plant in St. Louis, Arkansas, where James Smith McDonnell resided as chairman of the board and CEO. The then-seventy-four-year-old Donald Douglas Sr. was appointed honorary chairman of the board, while his then-forty-seven-year-old son continued to head the Douglas division of the company, based in Long Beach. The legendary patriarchal management style of McDonnell, who addressed his employees daily via a loudspeaker system installed in the factory, was retained by the new corporate entity: "This is Mac calling all the team" often resounded through the halls and offices of the McDonnell factory in St. Louis.

The in-flight profile of the first DC-8 models, -11 to -30. *Boeing*

The next major evolutionary step after the first three versions was the DC-8-50. *Boeing*

The DC-8-61 was much in demand, especially by North American carriers, who needed a larger aircraft for transcontinental routes. *Boeing*

The DC-8-63 was the final version of the great DC-8 series. SAS

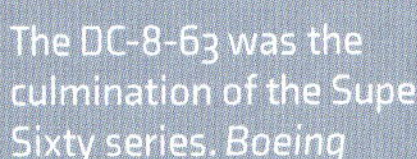

The DC-8-63 was the culmination of the Super Sixty series. *Boeing*

CHAPTER 3 TECHNICAL REFINEMENTS

The air intakes for the turbo-compressors, which provided cabin pressurization and ventilation, were located in the nose of the aircraft. They gave the DC-8 its characteristic "smile." *Orbis*

Close-up of the nose intakes of a Swissair DC-8. *ETH Zurich*

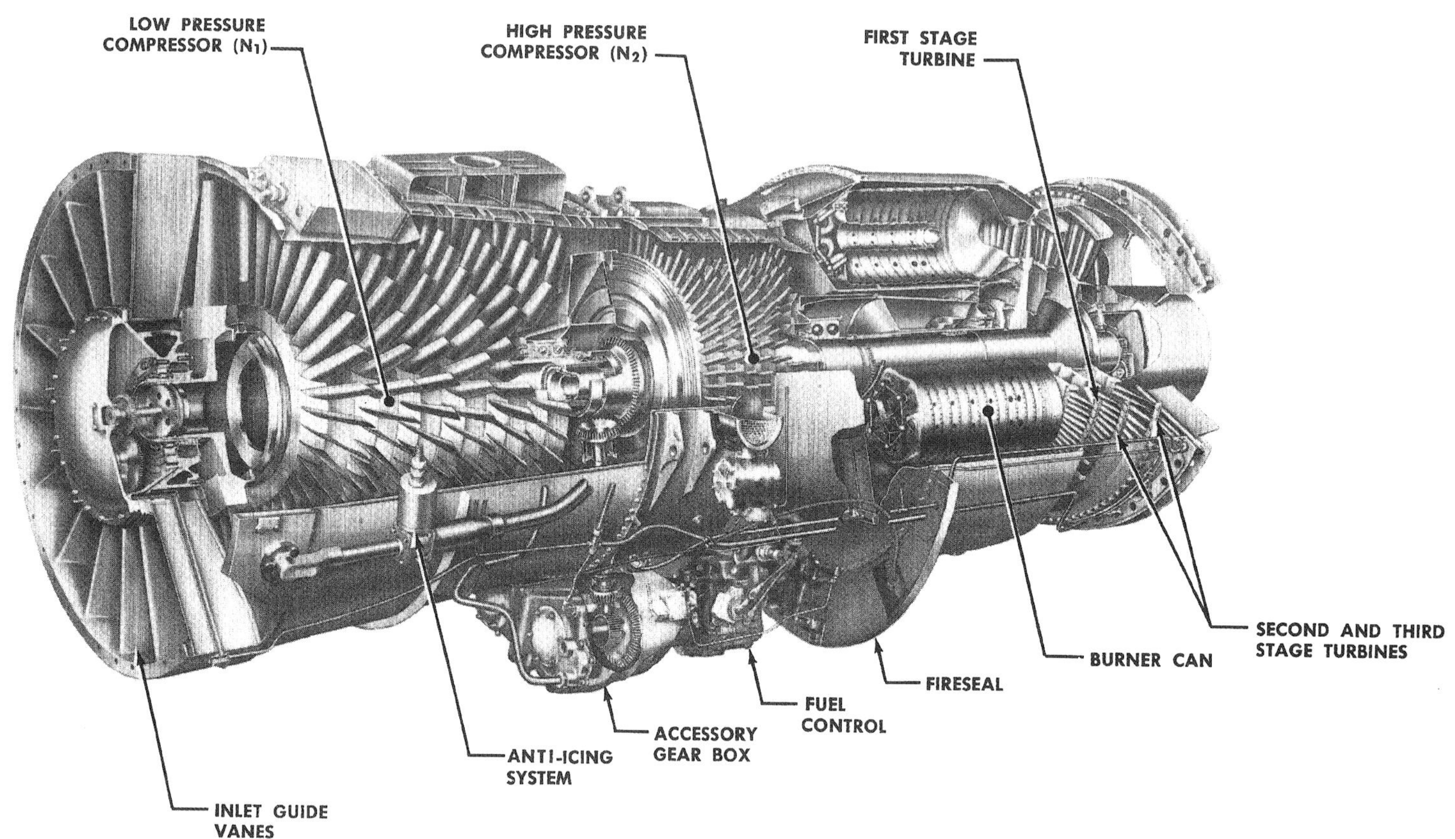

Cutaway drawing of a Pratt & Whitney JT4A engine from a Douglas DC-8 brochure produced in the summer of 1959. *Douglas / Marcus Kolskog collection*

HOW THE DC-8 GOT ITS "SMILE"

The DC-8 has some special technical features that set it apart from most other jets of its generation. For example, cabin pressurization was not generated directly by bleed air from the engines, but via a complicated process in the nose of the jet. Initially, it is the same as with modern jet engines: Bleed air is taken from a compressor stage of the DC-8's engines, and it in turn powers a turbine, which in turn is coupled to a compressor. This draws in the outside air and compresses it until the required cabin pressure is achieved. However, the military Pratt & Whitney J57 and J75 engines, which were the only power plants available for the DC-8 design, were not yet approved for this civil application. The risk seemed too great that the civil Pratt & Whitney JT3C-4 (J57) and JT4A-3 (J75) engines, which had been developed from them, would have leaking bearings whose oil vapors might contaminate the cabin air, an issue that has not lost its explosive nature to this day and has repeatedly led to health complaints from passengers and crew members! The air inlets for these four compressors installed in the nose gave the DC-8 its characteristic "smile."

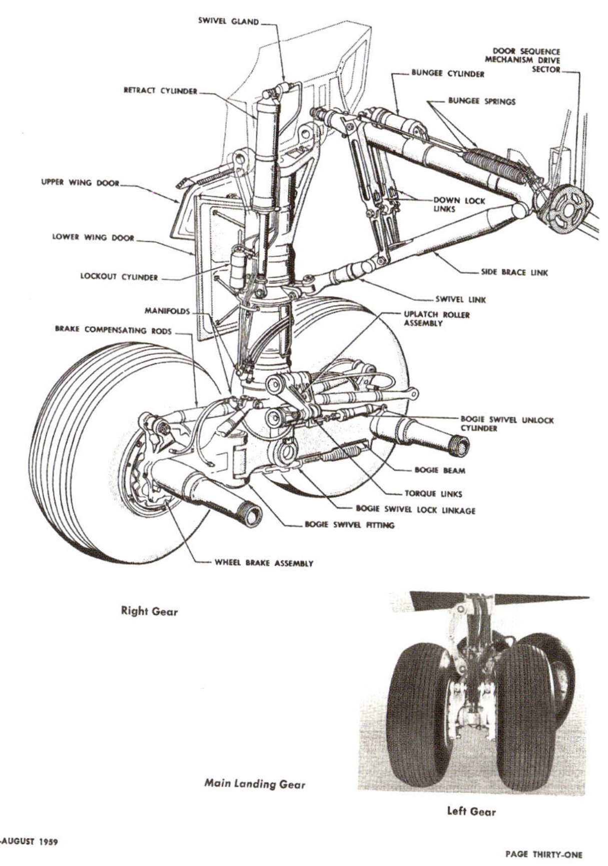

The main undercarriage of the first models of the DC-8 was steerable to reduce turning radius while navigating the ramps of airports. The early DC-8s also had a mechanism that allowed their engines to be started by using compressed air. *Douglas / Marcus Kolskog collection*

As a further curiosity, the first versions—up to and including the DC-8-50—also had hydraulically steerable main landing gear, which reduced the turning radius when maneuvering on small airport aprons. The landing gear of the DC-8 included another special feature. Engine number 3 could be started via the starboard main landing gear if no ground power unit was available. A pressure line was installed in the landing-gear leg, via which compressed air from the shock absorbers was fed into the engine, which could then be set in motion. The power for ignition of the combustion chambers was supplied by the onboard battery. Once engine number 3 was running, the other three engines were started by way of it. This was a procedure that was rarely used in practice and in which only one attempt was possible!

THE PALOMAR SEAT FOR THE DC-8

Douglas attached great importance to the design of the DC-8's cabin. Jack Graves had previously designed the interiors of all Douglas long-haul models before the big jet—starting with the DC-4. He came up with a progressive, modern concept for the DC-8 but also brought a touch of the old propeller era into the jet age. In theory, it would have been possible to fold down beds from the cabin ceiling on night flights, as in the "golden age of air travel." Like the propeller-driven airliners of the 1950s, such as the DC-4, DC-6, and DC-7, the first DC-8 versions also had curtains instead of sun shades on the cabin windows.

The Palomar seats of the DC-8-10, -20, -30, and -50 models were developed specially for the DC-8. *ETH Zurich*

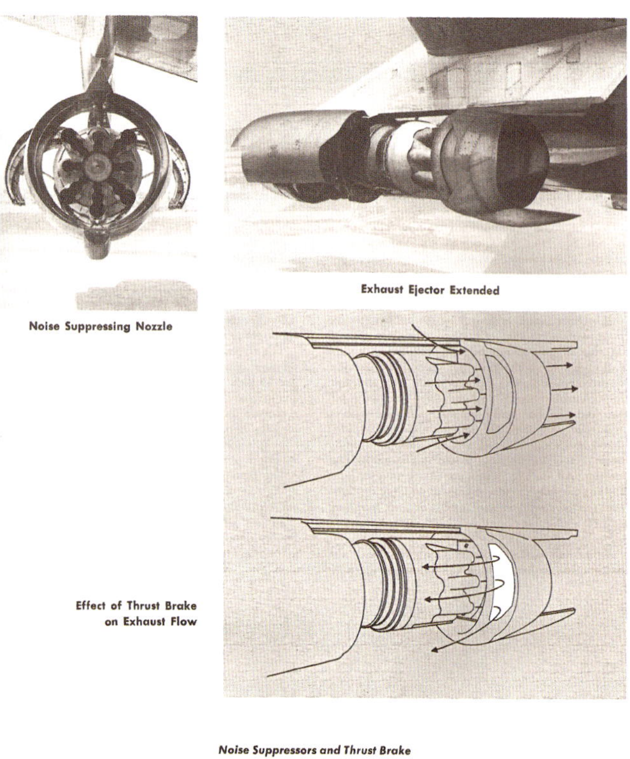

These drawings, taken from a Douglas brochure from 1959, illustrate how the thrust reversers operated. *Douglas / Marcus Kolskog collection*

Douglas had the Palomar passenger seat designed specially for the DC-8. It had all the standard fittings that are still used today, such as a fresh-air vent, call button for the cabin crew, folding table, and oxygen mask for emergencies. A fluorescent reading lamp was also attached to the side of each headrest. The individual rows of seats were attached to the cabin floor and to the side of the cabin wall. The supply lines for electricity and air ran through this lateral suspension. This meant that the rows of seats could be moved around the cabin or quickly replaced. Another curiosity: The armrest for the passengers sitting by the window was not attached to the individual seats, but to the side paneling. It ran lengthwise through the cabin in one piece from the first to the last row. Douglas patented the Palomar seat, which was installed in every DC-8 passenger jet up to the 50 series.

Compared to the Boeing 707, the DC-8 has relatively few—but larger—cabin windows. They have been optimized for the 40-inch (101.6 cm) distance between the seat backs. Douglas had modeled this on the first-class seating that was common on American airlines in the 1950s. What was well intentioned, however, led in later years, with much-higher-density seating, especially in economy class, to some window seats being closed off with no view of the outside—and thus causing frustration among passengers.

DEVELOPMENT OF THE THRUST REVERSER

One of the biggest challenges faced by the Douglas engineers when developing the DC-8 was the infernal noise emitted by the early Pratt & Whitney JT4A and Rolls-Royce Conway engines. The shrill "screech" caused by these engines resulted from the direct collision of the hot exhaust gases exiting the engines at high speed with the surrounding cold outside air. The Conway was a turbofan engine, in which air is directed past the outside of the engine core and envelops the hot air. However, its bypass ratio (i.e., the amount of air surrounding the hot-air jet) did not correspond in any way to the modern turbofan engines of our time.

In addition to the noise problem, there was still no experience with a thrust reverser that could be used to reduce the jet's speed in the air—but primarily to provide braking after touchdown upon landing. The task for the Douglas designers was therefore not only to reduce noise, but also to design a thrust reverser that could convert at least 40 percent of the thrust produced by the engines into braking energy.

To achieve the optimum result, Douglas tested a series of design drafts in wind tunnels as static models, scaled down and in original size. The developers quickly realized that much more work would have to be invested in the design of a suitable thrust reverser and noise enclosure than initially thought. The engineers saw the greatest challenge in designing a device that would not only be reliable in the hot engine gases, but also safe and durable.

In the end, two shapes emerged as suitable: scalloped nozzles and noise absorbers consisting of several tubes. Although they reduced the noise, the result was still not satisfactory. To solve this problem, Douglas invented the "ejector." It reduced the thrust loss during takeoff to an acceptable level. Wind tunnel tests also suggested that a scalloped design would be advantageous for the sound-absorbing nozzles. Supplementary investigations revealed the following picture, as Douglas wrote in its May–June 1959 issue of *Service Bulletin*: "For optimum sound reduction, a suppressing nozzle should have the following features: As large an outer diameter as possible at the exit plane. Lobes that increase in cross-sectional area with increase in radial distance from the thrust axis. No fewer than eight lobes. A relatively small center bullet. At least 90 percent of the exhaust area distributed in the lobes (10 percent or less of the exhaust area located in the annular passage around the bullet). Minimum thrust loss was also a major objective. To accomplish this, it was found that: The nozzle should have a cross-sectional flow area that is constant, or slightly converging, over most of its length. Convergence of the final flow area should take place rapidly in the final few inches of gas travel. The fewer the number of lobes, the less the thrust loss. Bullet size has little effect on static thrust of the nozzle."

The result of this research work can be admired on all DC-8 models, right up to the DC-8-40. The prototype lacked thrust reversers on its first flight. The striking ejector hangs from a suspension system installed below the firewall of the engine pylon. The vertical forces are dissipated via the structure of the pylon, while lateral stability is ensured by a link connected to the engine via a lower guide rail.

The thrust reverser is a so-called target type, with extending, shell-shaped thrust reversers that divert the exhaust gas flow forward.

A LITTLE ENGINE LORE

The military Pratt & Whitney J-57 engine is considered the forefather of all modern turbojet engines for jet airliners. The first versions of the Douglas DC-8 as well as those of the competing Boeing 707 were powered by the JT3, its civil variant. In the second half of the 1950s, this engine type was the only civil engine produced in the United States that was available with the required power output. In the military sector, the J-57 was used to power the eight-engine Boeing B-52 bomber, among other types.

The JT4A engine with extended ejector on an SAS DC-8-33 looks almost like a modern work of art in this photo from 1960. *SAS Museum*

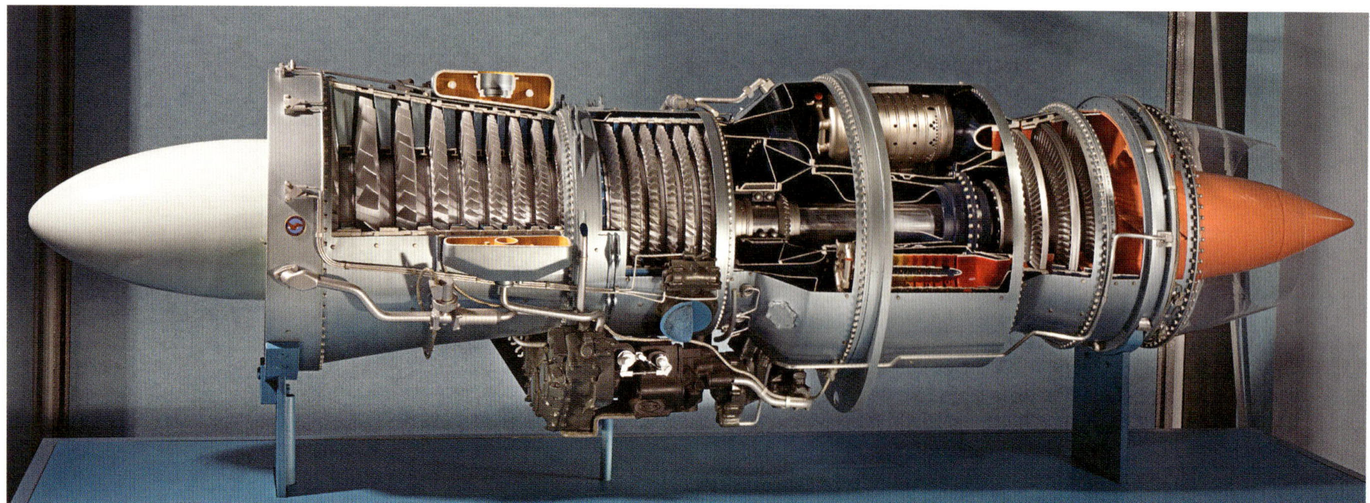

Cutaway model of a Pratt & Whitney JT3C, the civil version of the J-57 engine used by the military. It was the first type of engine used to power the DC-8. *National Air and Space Museum*

The JT3C was followed by the somewhat more powerful JT4A. What the two engines had in common was that they did not have the high bypass ratio that is common in modern-day turbofan engines.

This is a description published by Douglas of how the Pratt & Whitney JT4A worked:

> This engine is an axial-flow turbojet type with a fifteen[-]stage split compressor, an eight[-]can combustion chamber, and a three[-]stage split turbine. The axial-flow front, or low-pressure compressor, consists of an inlet guide vane and shroud assembly, seven stages of stator vanes, and a rotor having eight stages of blades.
>
> The front compressor is driven by the second[-] and third[-]stage turbines through the front compressor drive shaft. The axial-flow rear or high-pressure compressor consists of six stages of stator vanes and a rotor with seven stages of blades. The rear compressor is driven by the first[-]stage turbine through the rear compressor drive shaft. The purpose of the rear compressor is to further compress the air delivered by the front compressor and then feed this into the diffuser case and combustion chambers. Turbine nozzle assemblies direct exhaust gases at each of the turbines.
>
> The high-pressure compressor rotor rpm is "speed governed" by the engine fuel control. The low[-]pressure compressor is rotated by its turbines at whatever speed will ensure optimum flow through the compressor.
>
> The compressors deliver air to the combustion chamber under a maximum pressure ratio of approximately 12:1 under sea level static conditions. Fuel under pressure is sprayed into each of the eight burner cans through dual-orifice nozzles mounted in clusters of six at each burner inlet. Burner cans #4 and #5 are provided with igniter plugs for starting. When the fuel-air mixture is ignited, continuous combustion forces hot gases through the jet nozzle at the rear of the engine.

Characteristic air intake of a Pratt & Whitney JT4A engine on a DC-8-33. *SAS Museum*

The nozzle of a JT4A turbojet, designed to reduce engine noise. *SAS Museum*

THE FIRST TURBOFAN ENGINE

The British engine manufacturer Rolls-Royce took the significant evolutionary step toward today's turbofan engines with the world's first civil turbofan power plant, the Rolls-Royce Conway. Thanks to the fan, mounted at the front of the engine, it was more economical than pure turbojets.

This Rolls-Royce Conway turbofan engine is on display in the Royal Air Force Museum in Cosford. *Author's photo*

Deutsche Lufthansa, with the Boeing customer number 30, became the first customer for the Conway, which powered its Boeing 707s, now designated as the German airline's 430 version. Air Canada was the first DC-8 customer to use the Conway-12 in its Douglas jets. The first aircraft with this British engine was delivered to the airline as the DC-8-41 on September 25, 1960. CP Air, another Canadian airline, also chose Rolls-Royce as an engine supplier for its DC-8-43s. Another Rolls-Royce customer was Italy's Alitalia, which equipped its DC-8-42s with the engine.

The American answer to the Conway came in the form of the Pratt & Whitney JT3D turbofan engine, which became the standard power plant for all subsequent versions of the Boeing 707 and Douglas DC-8. This engine is based on the J-57 engine core, which is preceded by a two-stage fan with a bypass ratio of 1.43. The story of the JT3D is a typical episode of the time, when a manager's word counted for more than pages of contracts. Alarmed by General Electric's announcement that it was developing an economical and powerful GE CJ-805-23 turbofan engine for the projected Convair 990, Boeing feared that this might have an impact on orders for its 707 and 720 jet models. The decision to develop the JT3D was made over a few drinks on the sidelines of an aviation conference between Pratt & Whitney and Boeing in January 1958. A few days later, the engine manufacturer presented concrete performance data—and the rest is history. The powerful Pratt & Whitney fan engine, in particular, made the Boeing 707-320B and 720B superior to the CV 990 and forced Convair out of the civil aircraft market.

Both Boeing and Douglas engineers feared that the early Pratt & Whitney JT3C and JT4A and Rolls-Royce Conway engines had leaking bearings whose oil vapors could contaminate the cabin air and cause discomfort for both crew and passengers. For this reason, both the Boeing 707 and the Douglas DC-8 were equipped with special turbo compressors that built up the cabin pressure by compressing the ambient air. In the case of the 707, these compressors were located directly on the engine nacelles and could be recognized from the front by the small air intakes above the actual engine. The complex system of the early Douglas DC-8 compressors is explained in detail elsewhere. They were powered by compressed air from an engine compressor stage.

Cammacorp published this photo at the beginning of its program to convert the DC-8 to CFM56 power plants. *Cammacorp / Marcus Kolskog collection*

United Air Lines was the largest customer for the Cammacorp DC-8-70 program, purchasing twenty-nine aircraft. *Marcus Kolskog collection*

NASA's DC-8-72 begins its takeoff roll. The aircraft is no longer flying. *Dirk Grothe*

In contrast to the competing Douglas DC-8-71, -72, and -73 models, Boeing failed to launch a sustainable civil program to equip a version of the 707 with the GE/Snecma CFM-56 turbofan engine. Only a civil test aircraft known as the 707-700 and a few military KC-135 variants were equipped with the engine first offered for the Boeing 737-300 in the early 1980s, which temporarily became the standard engine for the 737 and Airbus A320 families. The program initiated by the Seven Q Seven consortium shortly after the turn of the millennium to retrofit 707-320Cs with quieter, more-powerful, and more-fuel-efficient Pratt & Whitney JT8D-219 engines was just as unsuccessful. The company, based in San Antonio, Texas, had to suspend its certification program for the aircraft marketed as the 707RE—which began in August 2001—after the attacks of September 11 and was unable to win any military or civilian customers in the years that followed.

WING RESEARCH

Although Boeing was ahead of the game with its Dash-80, 717, and 707 and was able to fall back on the results of the swept-wing research captured in Germany in 1945, Douglas did not allow itself to be put under pressure and invested time and money in an optimum design for the DC-8's wing. In addition to the basic requirements that had applied in the propeller era, such as high lift, good stall characteristics, stability, no flutter problems, and a design to accommodate wing tanks, a jet airliner's wing also must guarantee high Mach numbers in cruising flight. At the same time, however, it must also permit landing approaches at low speeds. The development of the DC-8 wing profile took place in cooperation with NASA in wind tunnels, in calculations by the Douglas engineering team, and as part of the analysis of military Douglas programs with swept wings. To achieve the greatest possible lift during takeoff and landing,

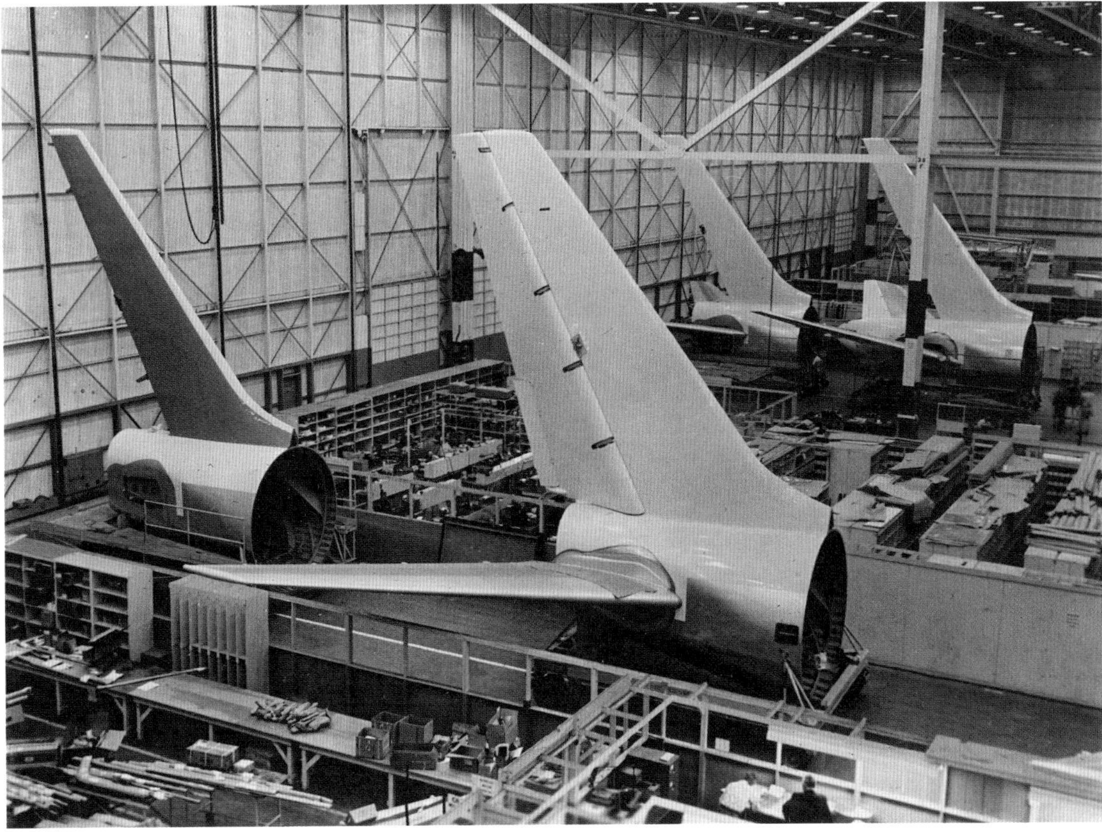
Assembly of DC-8 tail assemblies at Douglas in the late 1950s. *ETH Zurich*

the DC-8 wing is powerfully augmented by 30 percent chord, Douglas double-slotted flaps. This design represented a further improvement in the double-slotted, trailing[-] edge type of high[-]lift device pioneered by Douglas. By means of a special four-bar linkage, more chord extension is provided in the take-off setting, thereby giving greater lift. Because of the wing sweepback, each flap is divided into inboard and outboard sections interconnected to operate as a single unit. The flaps were hydraulically actuated.

The wing flaps are of all-metal construction, including the exhaust gate. The structure consists of a single spar, ribs, and aluminum alloy skin. The flaps incorporate all-metal airfoil vanes at the end of the edge, with aluminum alloy honeycomb cores.

The wing spoilers, of which there are five on each side, are all metal with aluminum alloy, honeycomb cores.

The ailerons are made in two sections—inboard and outboard. Their all-metal construction is conventional, with a single spar, ribs, a box-like leading edge, and a trailing edge.

To increase lift, each DC-8 wing is also equipped with two slots. The slots on the DC-8 are located near the leading

Douglas attached great importance to an aerodynamically sophisticated wing for its DC-8. *ETH Zurich*

edge of the wing and the engine pylons. Their extension mechanism is connected to that of the flaps via a linkage. In this way, the slots, in conjunction with the flaps, provide additional lift during takeoff and landing.

The DC-8 came late to the market, but Douglas achieved great success with it. The fact that, at the time of publication of this book, at least one of the 556 aircraft of all versions built between 1958 and 1972 is still in service as a freighter for charitable purposes speaks to its outstanding design.

CHAPTER 4 THE DC-8 COMES OF AGE

THE DEVELOPMENTAL HISTORY OF AN OUTSTANDING DESIGN

AN OVERVIEW OF THE VARIOUS VERSIONS OF THE DC-8 AND INDIVIDUAL AIRLINE DESIGNATIONS

DC-8 DOMESTIC	Early designation for what became the DC-8-11/-21
DC-8 INTERCONTINENTAL	Early designation for what became the DC-8-30/-40
DC-8B	Designation briefly used by Eastern Air Lines for its DC-8-21s
DC-8C	Designation used by Northwest, Japan Air Lines, and SAS for their DC-8-32s/-33s
DC-8-11	First production version for the launch customers Delta Air Lines and United Airlines, with Pratt & Whitney JT4A engines
DC-8-12	Further development of the DC-8-11 with wing slots and extended wingtips
DC-8-21	More powerful version ordered by Eastern Air Lines instead of the DC-8-11.
DC-8-31	
DC-8-30	With a maximum takeoff weight of 300,000 pounds
DC-8-32	
DC-8-30	With a maximum takeoff weight of 310,000 pounds. Long-range version flown by KLM, SAS, and Swissair.
DC-8-33	Improved version of the DC-8-32 with greater range
DC-8-41	The DC-8-40 for Trans-Canada Airlines, first user of this model
DC-8-42	DC-8-40 for Alitalia

DC-8-43	DC-8-40 for Canadian Pacific Airlines
DC-8-50/-51	The basic version of the DC-8 powered by Pratt & Whitney JT3D turbofan engines
DC-8-52/-53	Further development of the DC-8-50 with JT3D-3 engines, a leading edge increased in size by 4 percent and a higher maximum takeoff weight
DC-8-54 AF	Freight-only version, which was ordered only by United Airlines
DC-8-54 / -55 CF / JT	Douglas designation for all DC-8-54s in freight-only and combi versions
DC-8-55 AB	"Aft bulkhead" passenger version with rearward-offset, noncurved pressure bulkhead for additional rows of seats
DC-8-55 L	Passenger version without the rearward offset pressure bulkhead. The L stood for "less bulkhead."
DC-8F JET TRADER	Marketing designation for the DC-8-50CF

THE SUPER SIXTIES	
DC-8-61	Passenger version, first variant of the Super Sixty series
DC-8-61 F	Freighter version with side-mounted cargo door
DC-8-61 CF	Convertible version of the DC-8-61
DC-8-62	Passenger version of the DC-8-62
DC-8-62 AF	Freight-only version of the DC-8-62
DC-8-62 CF	Convertible version of the DC-8-62
DC-8-63	Passenger version of the DC-8-63
DC-8-63 AF	Freight-only version of the DC-8-63
DC-8-63 CF	Convertible version of the DC-8-63
DC-8-63 PF	Passenger version with strengthened undercarriage and cabin floor of the DC-8 AF and structural modifications to facilitate the installation of a side cargo door. Eastern Air Lines was the sole customer for this version and soon sold its aircraft to SAS.
CAMMACORP	
DC-8-71/-71F/-72/-72F/-73/-73F	Type designations corresponding to each of the DC-8-60 Super Sixty series

CHAPTER 5 THE DC-8 FREIGHTER: ENGINE OF GLOBAL TRADE

A BRIEF EXCURSION INTO THE HISTORY OF AIR FREIGHT

Air freight is more than transporting crates and pallets from point A to point B. It makes possible humanitarian-aid deliveries to crisis regions, is part of logistical supply chains, and, last but not least, facilitates the fastest possible delivery of temperature-sensitive goods around the world. In a nutshell: Air freight keeps the global economy running!

The Douglas DC-8 played its part early on. The first factory-built cargo version of the four-engine aircraft was the DC-8F-54, which was certified on January 29, 1963.

It was followed a year later by the DC-8F-55, which was certified on June 19, 1964. All versions of the DC-8 Super Sixty were available as freighters or combination passenger-freight versions from the factory, as were the seventy models retrofitted with CFM56 engines by Cammacorp.

It all started with the DC-8F Jet Trader cargo model, announced by company patriarch Donal Douglas Sr. during the rollout of the DC-8 prototype Ship One. It was based on the DC-8-50 and was Douglas's hope of securing a lucrative contract with the US military. This hope was soon dashed, but the concept of a freighter with a large side cargo hatch and reinforced cabin floor and aircraft structure remained. United Air Lines was the only customer for the DC-8-54AF all-cargo version, while Air Canada ordered the first DC-8-54CF Jet Trader combination version. Of the total of eighty-eight DC-8-50s delivered, fifteen were all-cargo aircraft without cabin windows and thirty-nine were passenger/cargo combos. The remaining aircraft left the Douglas factory as pure passenger aircraft.

In addition to United, customers for pure freight and combi versions included Seaboard World, KLM, SAS, Trans Caribbean, and Trans International. That Douglas had achieved a great success with the DC-8-50F can be seen from the fact that these aircraft continued to enjoy great popularity among smaller cargo carriers for many years after being retired by their original customers. Only the stricter noise regulations toward the end of the 1980s put an end to the use of DC-8-50 freighters in the United States and Europe.

Various versions of the DC-8-50, which differed in detail, became the first DC-8 freighters. Shown here is an SAS DC-8-55AF. *SAS Museum*

The DC-8-55AF was repainted after SAS designed a more modern version of its Viking theme in 1968. *Tom Weihe*

LAC was a Colombian passenger and freight airline that was founded in Barranquilla in 1974. Among other types, it operated the DC-8-55F on its freight network. *Author's collection*

The DC-8-54F shown here was delivered new by Douglas to Airlift International on June 17, 1964. In addition to this American cargo carrier, it was also flown by Japan Air Lines and Arrow Air. It was scrapped in Miami in August 1984, after twenty years of service. *Tom Weihe*

The appearance of the first DC-8 freighters on the world stage of air freight transport came at exactly the right moment. While the airfreight volume in 1960 was still 51,800 metric tons, it had already more than doubled to 122,900 tons by 1964. The next big leap, spurred on primarily by the first jet freighters, came just one year later, at 177,100 tons. This development was reflected in the global figures. In 1964 (excluding Russia and China), 2,585 billion air freight ton-miles were transported by air around the globe, rising to 3,405 billion air freight ton-miles a year later.

And something else contributed to the triumph of air freight: specially developed loading equipment, such as pallets and containers, as well as lifting platforms designed for air freight handling at airports. Jets were also fitted with rollers in the cargo floor for the first time, which made it much easier to move cargo shipments on board—and, together with other measures, significantly shortened the turnaround times of freighters compared to propeller-driven aircraft.

LN-PIP is the oldest DC-8 still in existence. It flew for the first time on July 2, 1960, and was delivered new to Pan Am as the Clipper Mandarin. Sold to Delta Air Lines in 1968, it was issued the new registration N8038A. In 1983 it was purchased by the company Chikko-Dan and was to be used to fly live chicks from Norway to Denmark. Just one year later, the dream came to an end. Chikko-Dan went bankrupt, and the aircraft was grounded at the SAS maintenance facility in Copenhagen. Since SAS was owed considerable sums for maintenance work that had not been paid for, SAS stripped the aircraft of all components that could be sold. Its last official registration was LN-PIR, but SAS jokingly changed it to "LN-PIP" in reference to its former chick transport role. To this day, this phony registration remains on the wreck, which for some years has been used as a training aid by the airport firefighting service. Dirk Grothe's photos show the aircraft just after it was taken out of service at Copenhagen, and in its current, very regrettable condition. *Dirk Grothe*

Of course, it was not only the DC-8-50F that contributed to this boom, but also the corresponding freighter and combi models of the Boeing 707 and the Vickers VC10. In addition, the CL-44, a large four-engine turboprop freighter produced by Canadair, and Douglas DC-4, DC-6, and DC-7 and Lockheed L-1049 and L-1649A, propeller-driven airliners converted into freighters, were also in large-scale use. The propeller-driven aircraft in particular, whose era came to an end far too early due to the early use of jets in passenger service—long before they were written off—experienced a renaissance in air freight operations.

However, it was the Douglas DC-8-63CF and -AF versions that brought the big breakthrough for aviation. Their payload of 110,000 pounds and range of 3,000 miles laid the foundation for today's logistics chains. The Boeing 747-200F wide-body freighter, available from 1972, set further standards in terms of payload and range. But that is another story.

Aviation photographer Dirk Grothe took this photo of this DC-8-55F operated by Trans Arabian Air Transport on June 25, 1987.

United Parcel Service (UPS) was the longtime operator of ten DC-8-71F and eighteen DC-8-73F freighters. *UPS*

A DC-8-73F of German Cargo Services on the ramp at Frankfurt/Main. *German Cargo*

McDONNELL DOUGLAS DC8-73F

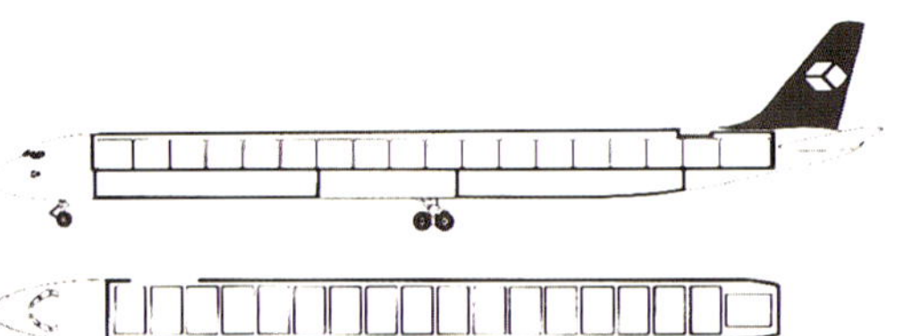

Aircraft:	McDonnell Douglas DC8-73F
Number:	5
Max. payload:	48.2 t
Max. available cargo space:	270 m³
Range with maximum payload:	5,200 km
Max. range with 25 t. payload:	8,900 km
No. of pallet positions:	18
Loadable containers:	see 3rd Register
DC8 Main Deck door dimensions:	Height 208 cm
	Width 356 cm

Please note that the dimensions of an item do not guarantee that the item can be loaded. This applies in particular to over-length items.

Cutaway drawing of the pallet and container positions of a German Cargo DC-8-73F and a list of its special loading equipment. Observant viewers will notice that German Cargo drew the cargo door on the main deck on the wrong side of the fuselage. *German Cargo*

A BRIEF DIGRESSION INTO THE HISTORY OF AIR FREIGHT

On September 19, 1783, the first "passengers" took to the skies in a man-made flying machine. Brothers Joseph Michel and Jacques Etienne Montgolfier launched their hot-air balloon, known as the Montgolfière, before the eyes of the French royal couple Louis XVI and Marie Antoinette in the courtyard of the Palace of Versailles, where it remained in the air for twelve minutes in front of the royal witnesses. For safety reasons, since the new technology was not yet fully trusted, there were no humans on board, but a sheep, a cockerel chicken, and a duck. With a twinkle in the eye, this successful flight experiment can be described as the birth of air freight.

While November 7, 1910, is considered the birth date of air freight in the United States, August 19, 1911, is the historically documented birth date of air freight in Europe. In the United States, a Wright Model B was used by Philip Orin Parmelee to fly 105 km (65 mi.) from Dayton to Columbus, Ohio, to deliver a package of silk in time for a planned business opening.

On the other side of the Atlantic, around nine months later, freshly printed copies of the daily newspaper *Berliner Morgenpost* were the first air freight to be flown from Berlin to Frankfurt an der Oder on board a Harlan monoplane. Company owner Wolfgang Harlan was originally a cab entrepreneur in Berlin when he teamed up with aircraft designer Karl Grulich to finance the production of the flying machine made of wood, fabric, and metal struts in Berlin-Johannisthal and market it under his own name. And another premiere took place at this traditional airfield in the German capital, when the world's first regulated airmail service, between Berlin and Weimar, was launched from there on February 5, 1919, using a Deutsche Luft-Reederei biplane.

All three events in 1783, 1910, and 1911 have a direct link to the present day. After all, both live animals and particularly urgent goods—who wants to open a store without goods or read yesterday's newspaper—as well as the transportation of letters and parcels are still among the cornerstones of modern air freight transport today. Whenever speed, security, and reliability are required within a transportation chain, air freight is usually the first choice. Logistics companies specializing in the transport of temperature-sensitive air freight, such as DHL, FedEx, and UPS, and international freight forwarders and cargo airlines such as Lufthansa Cargo are ideally prepared to transport millions of highly sensitive vaccines from manufacturers to regional vaccination centers as part of a global logistics cold chain for perishable products.

The express freight service TNT also used DC-8-73Fs on its worldwide freight network. *TNT*

This SAS DC-8-62AF, registered LN-MOC and named Kettil Viking, was operated by Thai Airways International from April 1979 with the registration HS-TGS. SAS

This photo shows the former Kettil Viking in Thai livery with the registration HS-TGS. *Tom Weihe*

CHAPTER 6
THE DC-8 IN SERVICE AROUND THE WORLD

African Safari Airways (ASA): Founded in 1967, African Safari Airways was part of the African Safari Club Group of companies. The airline operated charter flights from European hub airports primarily to its operational base in Mombasa, Kenya. African Safari was once the largest holiday company in the East African country, with airlines, cruise ships, lodges, and hotels. The airline started flying with Bristol Britannia turboprops, followed by the DC-8 as the longest-operated aircraft type in the history of ASA. A Douglas DC-10-30 was followed by an Airbus A310-300 as the last flown type, when the company ceased operations in 2009.

ASA was a Kenyan charter airline with headquarters in Mombasa and was part of the Swiss tour operator African Safari Club. As its name suggests, it was used mainly for tourist flights between Europe and Kenya. Founded in 1967, the airline ceased operations in 2008. *Dirk Grothe*

Air Afrique

Founded in 1961 in Abidjan, the capital of Côte d'Ivoire (Ivory Coast), Air Afrique ceased operations in 2001, its fortieth year of existence. As the name suggests, Air Afrique was not a national airline, but an alliance of airlines and West African states. On the airline side, Air France and UTA, also French, were involved. In addition to DC-8s, Air Afrique initially flew Boeing 707s and S.E. 210 Caravelles. *ETH Zurich*

Air Canada: Air Canada is Canada's largest airline and the largest provider of scheduled passenger services in the Canadian market, the Canada-US transborder market, and the international market to and from Canada. Air Canada is a founding member of Star Alliance, providing one of the world's most comprehensive air transportation networks. Air Canada's predecessor, Trans-Canada Air Lines (TCA), inaugurated its first flight on September 1, 1937. The fifty-minute flight aboard a Lockheed L-10A carried two passengers and mail between Vancouver and Seattle. By 1964, TCA had grown to become Canada's national airline; it changed its name to Air Canada. The airline became fully privatized in 1989. Its corporate headquarters are located in Montreal. The airline operated the DC-8 in both the cargo and passenger versions and various DC-8 subtypes.

Air India Cargo: Air India was founded in 1932 by Jenhangir Ratanji Dadabhoy Tata as Tata Aviation Services in Bombay. It began operations with a de Havilland D.H.80 Puss Moth on October 15, 1932. In 1946, it became a public limited company and changed its name to Air India. The company flew Douglas DC-3 and Vickers Viking aircraft on domestic routes and, from April 1948, Lockheed L-749s on the airline's international route network. In the jet age, Air India operated mainly Boeing 707 and 747 jets. However, it also flew Lockheed L-1011 Tristars and a Douglas DC-8-63AF freighter leased from Cargolux with the registration LX-BCV.

Air New Zealand: On April 1, 1965, New Zealand's international airline, Tasman Empire Airways Limited (TEAL), was renamed Air New Zealand Limited. The New Zealand, United Kingdom, and Australian governments had

Trans-Canada Airlines (TCA), which was renamed Air Canada in 1965, was an early buyer of the DC-8. Its first aircraft bore the construction number 9. It ordered both the passenger versions of the Douglas jet as well as its freight variant, the DC-8-55F Jet Trader. TCA was one of the few airlines to select the Rolls-Royce Conway engine for its DC-8-41s, -42s, and -43s. It also acquired the DC-8-54JT, -61, and -63 versions. The photo depicts a Jet Trader being readied for flight. *Air Canada*

Photographer Dirk Grothe captured TF-BCV, which had been leased from Cargolux, at Frankfurt/Main on June 26, 1983. *Dirk Grothe*

established TEAL in 1939 to provide a Trans-Tasman air link. TEAL's Auckland–Sydney flights began in April 1940, using Short S30 Empire flying boats. For twenty years, TEAL's flying boats provided a memorable spectacle as they took off and landed near city centers. The renowned 1950s Coral Route from Auckland to Fiji, Samoa, the Cook Islands, and Tahiti contributed its own distinctive legends. A conversion to land-based planes began in 1954, when the popular Auckland–Sydney service switched to Douglas DC-6 aircraft. In 1960, land-based planes also took over the Coral Route. New Zealand assumed full ownership of TEAL in April 1961. In 1947 the government had established the New Zealand National Airways Corporation (NAC), which became the country's primary domestic carrier. In April 1978, NAC merged with Air New Zealand. The enlarged Air New Zealand was the first local airline to offer both international and domestic services. The Douglas DC-8 was the first long-distance jet airliner operated by Air New Zealand, to be followed by the McDonnell Douglas DC-10-30 and Boeing 747.

Air New Zealand handed out postcards like this one on its DC-8-52s. *Air New Zealand / author's collection*

Air Spain

Air Spain was a Spanish charter flight company based on the island of Mallorca. Between 1971 and 1975, it operated DC-8-21s such as aircraft EC-CAD, shown here. It was photographed by Tom Weihe in Copenhagen on April 16, 1974. Named Isla de Tenerife, the DC-8-21 had originally been delivered to Eastern Air Lines in 1960. Air Spain ceased operations because of financial difficulties in 1975. *Tom Weihe*

Alitalia: Alitalia (Società Aerea Italiana S.p.A.) was founded in 1946. For decades it served as the Italian flag carrier, with its main base in Rome. It had a close relation with Douglas, and later McDonnell Douglas. Operated aircraft types made in Long Beach ranged from the DC-8 to the DC-9, DC-10, MD-80, and, finally, MD-11. On October 10, 2020, the Italian government signed a decree to allow the reorganization of the airline as ITA: Italia Trasporto Aereo S.p.A. This successor to Alitalia was acquired by the Lufthansa Group in early 2025.

This DC-8-42/43 with the registration I-DIWE was christened Christophoro Columbus, a name that was untended to evoke wanderlust. The Italian national airline Alitalia was a loyal Douglas customer and, in addition to the DC-8, operated various versions of the DC-9, DC-10, and MD-11 jetliners on its extensive route network. This photo was taken on March 9, 1967, at Alitalia's home airport of Rome-Fiumicino. *Tom Weihe*

Arista

On January 23, 1983, the American airline Arista International leased the DC-8-62 with the registration OY-KTE from the Scandinavian airline SAS. The photo was taken at Copenhagen-Kastrup on November 23 of that year, ten days after the aircraft was returned to SAS. In addition to OY-KTE, Arista also leased the DC-8-62s SE-DDU and SE-DBI from SAS. Arista was founded in 1981 and began operations in April 1982. It ceased operations in 1984. *Tom Weihe*

Atlantis: Atlantis was a German holiday carrier, operating in the late 1960s and early 1970s. Their medium-range fleet consisted of DC-9-30s and DC-8-30s, acquired by Swissair, plus DC-8-63s, purchased directly from Douglas, for long-distance routes. Atlantis challenged Lufthansa on transatlantic flights between West Germany and the United States but failed to receive the necessary traffic rights for scheduled services from the German government. The planned introduction of DC-10-30 had to be canceled, and Atlantis went out of business in 1972.

Atlantis was a reliable German vacation airline that was popular with passengers, but ultimately unsuccessful. It was founded in 1968 by former employees of Südflug and operated the DC-8-63CF pictured here on long-haul flights to the United States. This—and two other DC-8-63CFs—were received from Douglas brand new. Two DC-8-32/33s were also used by the airline. In particular, ruinous competition with Lufthansa on the routes to North America ultimately led to bankruptcy in October 1972. *Atlantis / author's collection*

Aviaco

Overseas National Airways, Martinair Holland, KLM, and even Iran Air flew this DC-8-55F for a short time before it was purchased by Aviaco, a subsidiary of the Spanish airline Iberia, on September 30, 1977. It operated in the airline's colors until July 1985. Dirk Grothe photographed the DC-8 at Frankfurt/Main on June 22, 1984. *Dirk Grothe*

Braniff: Brothers Paul and Thomas Braniff founded Braniff Airways as an Aero Club in Oklahoma City in 1927. The airline quickly grew thanks to Douglas DC-3, DC-4, and DC-6 propliners. Braniff developed a strong network, primarily domestic and from the United States to Latin America. Lockheed L-188 Turboprops, Boeing 727, BAC 1-11, and Douglas DC-8 took Braniff into the jet age. The US artist Alexander Calder was hired in 1972 to create the most prominent livery of any Douglas DC-8. Braniff was famous for its flying color billboard liveries in various green, blue, red, turquoise, brown, and orange tones. Global fame reached its "Big Orange" Boeing 747. Saluting the space age, beginning in the late 1960s, Braniff even designed a space uniform for its cabin attendants.

This scale model of a DC-8-62 was a gift from the airline Braniff to the National Air and Space Museum. The model is painted in the then-sensational livery created by the American artist Alexander Calder. Braniff hired him to create this flying work of art to promote air travel to Latin America. *National Air and Space Museum*

Capitol

Douglas delivered this DC-8-63CF brand new to Capitol International Airways on August 20, 1968. Other operators of this jet were Overseas National Airways, Icelandair, Evergreen International Airlines, and United Parcel Service (UPS). The latter had it converted into a DC-8-73 in November 1984 and operated it with the registration N867UP. *Dirk Grothe*

This DC-8-62, N924CL, of Capitol International Airways, was photographed at Frankfurt/Main in 1984. It had originally carried the registration HB-IDL and had been named Aargau by Swissair. Douglas delivered the DC-8 to Swissair on February 6, 1972. Subsequent operators of this Super Sixty were National Airlines, Eagle Air, and Airborne Express, where it bore the registration N802AX. *Dirk Grothe*

This DC-8-61 with the registration N8765 completes the Capitol trio in this book. It was delivered by Douglas to Eastern Air Lines on November 15, 1968. It also flew in the colors of Overseas National Airways, Saudia, Air Niger, Airlift International, Spantax, and Atlanta Icelandic. *Dirk Grothe*

Cargolux: Cargolux Airlines International S.A. began its flight operations at Luxembourg Capital Airport in 1970. After the first Canadair CL-44 long-haul freighters, with turboprop engines and "swing tails" for easier cargo loading, it consistently opted for the Douglas DC-8-63. "Speed was the name of the game," and so the DC-8 was Cargolux's economic answer to the challenges of the air freight market. In 1973, the airline opted for the cargo version of the Super Sixty. For the first time, the Luxembourg–Hong Kong–Luxembourg route could be covered in under thirty-two hours. As the airline writes in its history, the DC-8 was the key to expanding the Cargolux network to other destinations. In addition to its own route network, Cargolux also leased DC-8-63s to other airlines, such as Flying Tiger. Some aircraft were also converted for temporary passenger transportation on Hajj pilgrimage flights to Mecca. Today, Cargolux operates only Boeing 747-400F and 747-8F wide-body freighters, the first of which joined the fleet in 1993 and 2011.

Condor: In the summer months of 1985 and 1986, the vacation airline Condor, then a wholly owned subsidiary of the Lufthansa Group, leased a McDonnell Douglas DC-8-73CF from the Lufthansa cargo subsidiary German Cargo Services (GCS) for passenger flights. The aircraft was flown by GCS cockpit crews and, before it began transporting passengers, was fitted out with a comfortable passenger cabin with 252 seats, in line with Condor standards. The large, deactivated cargo door on the main deck was the only reminder of its original purpose as a carrier of air freight consignments on behalf of the Lufthansa Group. The aircraft, with the registration D-ADUC, was originally manufactured in 1969 as a DC-8-63CF for the American cargo airline Seaboard World and in 1983 was converted by Cammacorp into the DC-8-73CF version, with quieter and more-economical CFM-56-1C engines.

The DC-8-54F pictured here had an eventful history. Originally delivered to Trans-Canada Airlines (TCA) with the registration CF-TJL on April 24, 1963, it was later operated by Cargolux, ARCA Colombia, Taino Airlines, and Andes Airlines after being sold to the Loch Ness Company in December 1984. The photo shows it in July 1985 at Luxembourg Airport—Cargolux's home base. *Dirk Grothe*

The German vacation airline Condor leased a DC-8-73F freighter, which had been converted into a passenger aircraft, from German Cargo for two summers. *Dirk Grothe*

Cubana

On October 6, 1976, this Cubana DC-8-43 fell victim to a terrorist attack, in which all on board were killed. Five minutes after taking off from Bridgetown, Barbados, two time bombs exploded in the cabin. Initially, the captain managed to steer the plane back to Bridgetown, but then the jet crashed into the sea in flames. All seventy-three people on board died. *Clint Groves, GNU Free Documentation License, Version 1.2*

Delta Air Lines: Delta took delivery of its first DC-8-11 on July 22, 1959. It is not often that a speed record is set on the very first day—but that is what happened on that day in July. Bearing the registration N801E, Ship 801 covered the 2,497-mile distance from the Douglas factory in Long Beach to Miami in four hours and forty-three minutes. This beat the previous record from the American West Coast to the East Coast, set by a Douglas DC-7, by one hour and seven minutes. The record-breaking crew of the DC-8-11 consisted of Captain T. P. "Pre" Ball, superintendent of flight operations; Captain W. Lee McBride, chief pilot Miami/Dallas; and Captain James H. Longino, assistant chief pilot, Atlanta.

The fact that Miami was chosen as the destination for the DC-8's maiden flight, and not the Delta hub in Atlanta, was undoubtedly a dig at Eastern Air Lines. It was supposed to receive the fourteenth DC-8 to be built but hesitated to wait for more-powerful engines to become available. So, it was up to Delta to advertise the advantages of jet air travel to the traveling public in Florida.

Delta arranged for a "Jetway" passenger pier to be installed at the terminal for the start of scheduled flights with the DC-8 in Atlanta—a trend that continued at airports around the world with the dawn of the jet age.

And Delta celebrated another premiere at the same time as the introduction of its Douglas four-engine aircraft. In the summer of 1959, it presented the "widget" logo on its DC-8-11s for the first time as the trademark of the Royal Jet Service, which was adopted by the entire fleet and for years was the familiar symbol of Delta Air Lines.

Not in perfect condition, but original. Depicted in this photo is a postcard that was given to passengers on Delta Air Lines' DC-8-11s. *Delta Air Lines / Marcus Kolskog collection*

Ship 801 was the first DC-8 to be used in passenger service anywhere in the world. Delta Flight 823 departed New York International Airport (Idlewild) at 9:20 on the morning of September 18, 1959, for a flight to Atlanta. The fact that Delta was first and not United Air Lines, which also introduced the DC-8 on that day, was due to the time difference between New York and Chicago—the departure airport of the first United flight.

The interior of the Delta DC-8-11 was created by Douglas designers in collaboration with Delta. Its colors are said to have been inspired by the sky and the sea. Alluding to this, the cabin ceiling had a design called Cosmos, showing stars and planets.

Delta Air Lines used advertising brochures like this one to promote flights aboard its new DC-8 jetliners. *Delta Air Lines*

The beginning of a wonderful new chapter in your life

Once you've flown a Delta DC-8 jet you'll find yourself wedded to this wonderful new type of travel.

The DC-8 is the world's newest, most advanced jetliner and the largest ever to bear the Douglas name. Whether you travel deluxe first class or thrifty supercoach, you'll be impressed with the spaciousness and extra room per passenger. Aisles are ample, seats broad and ceilings sweep wide overhead.

In a cabin filled with soft music by Muzak, rich paneling and modern plastics contrast with soft leather, thick carpeting and colorful drapes and curtains, under the restraint of indirect lighting. The rich, new colors and textures combine to tell you that a magnificent travel experience awaits you.

The DC-8 is the first jetliner to be planned exclusively for passenger use from its inception ... 3½ years ahead in engineering and decor.

A NEW EXPERIENCE IN QUIET, VIBRATION-FREE FLIGHT

Spanning the full width of the huge fuselage is a seven-seat lounge adjoining the cabin for first class passengers. Here one finds an atmosphere of rich informality—a table for cards or conferences—in an area of unusual quiet, completely free of engine or propeller vibration.

This absence of vibration, even at speeds of nearly 10 miles a minute, is one of the unique characteristics of jetliner travel. Inner tensions vanish with the vibration. You experience a degree of relaxation comparable only to that associated with your own easy chair.

Menu to match the magnificence of design

Special cuisine and complimentary champagne

MENU

CHAMPAGNE SERVICE
Fresh Gulf Shrimp Cocktail
Remoulade Sauce
CHARCOAL-BROILED TENDERLOIN STEAK
to your order or
ROCK CORNISH HEN
(Seafood Entrée available on appropriate days)
Stuffed Baked Potato—Cheddar
Green Beans Almondine
Royal Chef's Salad—Honey French Dressing
Hot Rolls and Butter Individual Fruit Pie
Coffee, Tea, Milk
Mints—Cigarettes

A completely new dining service matches the advanced design of Delta's new DC-8 Jets.

A large and substantial table not only folds down but slides toward you for ideal positioning. The dinner tray itself is of exclusive design, accommodating new free-form, dual-toned *Melamine* service ware.

Menus will vary with the season and the region, and deluxe luncheons and dinners are preceded by champagne service, *compliments de la maison*. Cocktails and highballs are also available at a modest tariff on all first class Royal Jet flights. Individual breakfast and afternoon snack trays plus assorted beverages are served at appropriate times in the first class section.

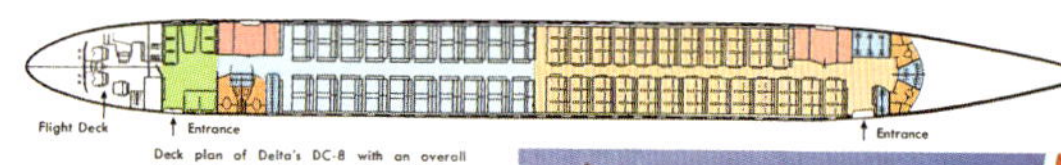

Deck plan of Delta's DC-8 with an overall fuselage length of 146 ft. and width of 12 ft. 3 in.

Deluxe first class cabin — Lounge
Supercoach cabin — Galley areas
Lavatories — Coat racks

All DC-8's Radar-equipped

The giant size of the DC-8 has to be seen to be appreciated. The cabin floor is on a second story level; the fin and rudder soar four stories into the air. One of the horizontal tail surfaces would make the wing of a small plane. Even the huge DC-6's and DC-7's begin to look small when they park beside this new Queen of the Skyways.

Deluxe

Miss Edith Head, Fashion Chief for Paramount Pictures, winner of six Oscars for her film-featured creations, and author of the current best seller, "The Dress Doctor."

THE FORW

DELTA

JET AGE INSPIRES NEW COSTUME DESIGN FOR STEWARDESSES

Delta's transition into the Jet Age is not alone a technical one. To design a smart new uniform for the elite corps of young women selected to serve in the new DC-8's, Delta turned to famed Hollywood fashion designer Edith Head.

The result is this handsomely tailored one-piece costume in honey beige which Miss Head calls the "Jet Jumper." The *jet flame* scarf is inspiring a new line of cosmetics. A short box jacket converts it to a suit for Terminal wear, while for blustery days there is a dashing beige leather top coat to complete the ensemble.

Four stewardesses are assigned to the big new jets, two serving in first class and two in the supercoach section.

Blue uniforms in other photos are standard on Delta's piston engine fleet.

THE DC-8 and should no called "prop- aircraft whic A TRUE JE far faster an features resp

Deluxe First Class — A NEW EXPERIENCE IN TRAVEL LUXURY

THE FORWARD CABIN features wide aisles and new "unitized" seating with over-the-shoulder lights for reading at any angle of recline, foot hassocks, fold-out tables and lights for writing or dining. Air vent and call button are at finger-tip command.

FIRST CLASS LOUNGE is the scene for a demonstration of the remarkable vibration-free characteristics of the smooth-flying DC-8, as children play with balancing block game in an atmosphere of quiet and comfort. Cruising almost 600 miles an hour at 30,000 ft. in the realm of jets, most weather is left far below.

Royal JET Service

ARRIVE REFRESHED AFTER A VIBRATION-FREE FLIGHT

THE DC-8 IS A TRUE JET and should not be confused with so-called "prop-jet" or "jet-powered" aircraft which employ propellers. A TRUE JET, like the DC-8, is far faster and has none of the features responsible for vibration.

THE DRIVING FORCE in one of Delta's DC-8 true jets comes from the reaction to the exhaust blasts (red arrow) of its four smooth-turning turbines and amounts to 52,000 lbs. thrust at take-off. These engines have had more than 1,000,000 hours of military and commercial use and are considered among the most reliable aircraft power units ever built. External noise is largely controlled by design of exhaust outlets and by a suppressor ring which encircles exhaust blast at take-off.

Thrifty Supercoach — SAME SPEED WITH UP TO 28% SAVING IN FARE

SUPERCOACH SEATS are also of the "unitized" design with built-in features similar to those in the deluxe section. Tables fold out from back of seat ahead and slide toward passenger. Complimentary hot meals are served to supercoach patrons at appropriate times in flight.

AIRFOAM-CUSHIONED contour seats recline throughout a wide range of angles without affecting folding tables. Cool fluorescent over-the-shoulder reading lights are in correct position for any desired angle of the seat. All accessories are within easy finger-reach.

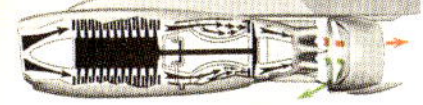

To slow down the jetliner on landing, the pilot employs a reverse-thrust mechanism which swings in behind the exhaust blast and deflects it forward (green arrow). This has the same effect as reversing the propellers and saves excessive brake and tire wear. In flight, the reversing mechanism fits snugly into the nacelle ahead of the exhaust stacks. Engines burn kerosene and four of them consume as much air in cruising as is inhaled by a city of 1¼ million inhabitants.

Delta ship numbers 800 to 821 (N801E–N806E) were delivered as DC-8-11s and subsequently upgraded to the standard of the DC-8-12 and finally the DC-8-51. All DC-8-11s except for Ship 800, which Delta took over from Trans International Airlines, came brand new from Douglas in Long Beach. Delta also acquired seven DC-8-33s from Pan Am in December 1968 and August 1969, which were used as part of a Delta-Pan Am interchange service to Europe and other selected long-haul destinations. They flew until they were sold to Boeing in January 1974.

On April 18, 1967, the first Delta DC-8-61 took off on a scheduled flight. Despite having 60 percent more seats than the standard DC-8, its operating costs were only 10 percent higher. Although they were certified for 252 passengers, Delta used its Super Sixties in a two-class configuration with only 195 seats.

Between April 1982 and November 1983, Delta upgraded its DC-8-61s to DC-8-71 standard with four General Electric / Snecma CFM56-1 engines. On April 24, 1982, Delta celebrated another world premiere when flight 910 became the world's first DC-8-71 to take off from Atlanta on a commercial flight. The destination of the premiere was Savannah, Georgia. The conversion to DC-8-71 standard included not only the replacement of the engines, but also a completely new interior, new air-conditioning in the cabin, and an upgrade of the cockpit. For each of the thirteen aircraft, Delta invested 42,000 working hours by its Technical Operations Center in Atlanta. The result was worth it, since the modified DC-8-71s were around 13 decibels quieter and consumed 20 percent less fuel than the DC-8-61.

The aircraft were sold to the express freight service United Parcel Service (UPS) in December 1986 and initially leased back. The DC-8 chapter of Delta Air Lines ended only on May 1, 1989, after more than twenty-nine years, with the retirement of the last two DC-8-71s remaining in the fleet. Forty-two DC-8s of the -11, -12, or -51 versions (twenty-two); -33 version (seven); and -61/-71 (thirteen) version were flown by Delta during this period.

Eastern Air Lines: The long-established airline based in Miami, Florida, was the launch customer for this early version of the DC-8, of which it ordered sixteen. They were delivered starting in October 1960 and remained in the fleet until 1973–74. The first aircraft delivered wore a red, white, and blue "Fly Eastern's Golden Falcon" livery. This slogan was changed to "Fly Eastern Air Lines" in 1960. From the mid-1960s, Eastern painted its DC-8-21s with the legendary field hockey stick logo. DC-8-51, -61, and DC-8-63PF versions complemented the early DC-8s with short fuselage.

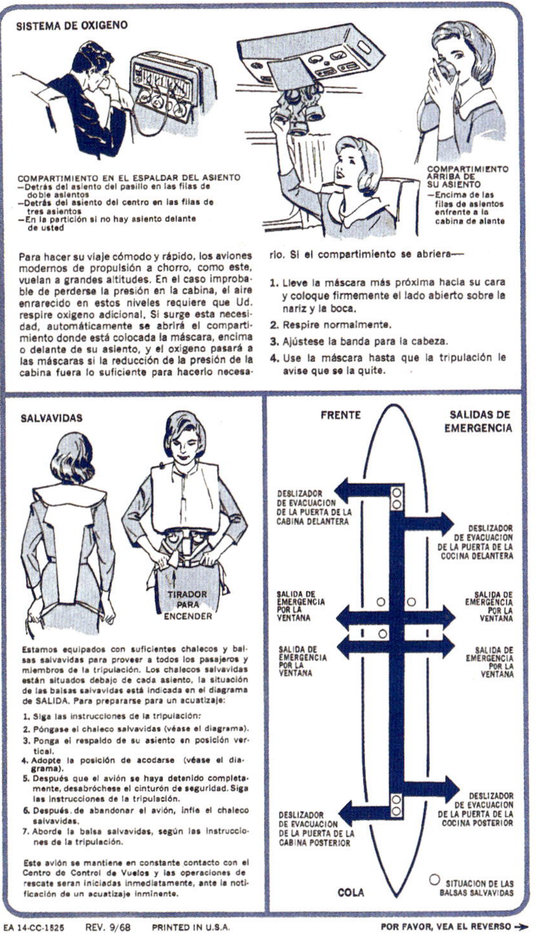

The front and reverse of a safety card for the DC-8-21s flown by Eastern Air Lines

Finnair: Finnair is one of the world's oldest operating airlines. Since it was founded in 1923 as Aero OY, the company has grown from a small airline to a strong and respected member of the international airline industry. In 1960, Aero OY became the first small airline to enter the jet age, with its new S.E. 210 Caravelle passenger jets. The first jet routes were Helsinki–Copenhagen–Cologne–Frankfurt and Helsinki–Stockholm–Oslo. Later the Caravelles were also used on flights to Hamburg, Amsterdam, London, Paris, Zurich, and Malmö. In 1968, Finnair revealed its new logo and made the name change from Aero OY official. During the same year, Finnair carried one million passengers for the first time. Flights from Helsinki to New York via Copenhagen and Amsterdam began in May 1969. The route was operated with DC-8 aircraft that Finnair had acquired earlier that year. Finnish designer Tapio Wirkkala's glassware Ultima Thule was introduced on Finnair's New York route. The classic design is still being used today in Finnair business class.

Like SAS, the national airline of Finland in northern Europe was a longtime operator of the DC-8. When Tom Weihe photographed the DC-8-62 OH-LFY at Copenhagen on July 29, 1973, the aircraft was wearing markings commemorating the fiftieth anniversary of the airline's founding. *Tom Weihe*

Nocturnal loading of freight onto a DC-8-63F of Flying Tiger Line at Zurich airport. *ETH Zurich*

Flying Tiger Line: The first aircraft type operated by the Flying Tiger Line, which was founded by Robert W. Prescott and Sam Mosher on June 25, 1945, under the name National Skyways Freight Corporation, was a Budd RB-1 Conestoga. Built entirely of stainless steel, this type was decommissioned after a short period of service with the military, and the seventeen examples built were sold to the then-new freight line.

The ungainly looking Budd RB-1 Conestoga was the first type operated by the new airline Flying Tiger Line. *Flying Tiger Line*

According to the founder of the Flying Tiger Line, American air traffic controllers often made fun of this bulky freighter, following the official takeoff clearance with the words "Go ahead, if you think it will be okay." A single Budd RB-1 has been preserved and can be viewed at the Pima Air Museum in Tucson, Arizona.

In 1946, the airline was renamed Flying Tiger Line, since many former pilots of the First American Volunteer Group (AVG), known as the Flying Tigers, joined the airline. The airline with the nickname Tiger operated Douglas DC-3s, C-54s, and DC-6s as well as Curtiss C-46 Commandos and Lockheed L-1049 Super Constellations before putting the first large turboprop aircraft into service in 1961 with the Canadair CL-44. The real breakthrough in the air freight industry came with all-cargo freighters such as the DC-8-63AF/CF of the Flying Tiger. They were capable of carrying a payload of 110,000 pounds at a speed of 550 miles per hour over a range of 3,000 miles. The DC-8-63 freighters enabled Flying Tiger, for example, to set up daily international freight line services between the United States and the most-important Asian markets. From 1978, Flying Tiger acquired shares in competitor Seaboard World Airlines until it took over the latter completely on October 1, 1980. For a time, Flying Tiger was the largest cargo airline in the world.

The elegant DC-8-63Fs were operated by Flying Tiger from 1968—and converted DC-8-73Fs until they were taken over by Federal Express at the end of 1988.

German Cargo Services: In 1977, Deutsche Lufthansa founded German Cargo Services GmbH (GCS) in Frankfurt as a new air freight subsidiary. Lufthansa itself flew air freight shipments either in the underfloor cargo hold of its passenger aircraft or on board its 747-230 Combis. The airline also used Boeing 707-330 and 747-230 all-cargo freighters for scheduled freight services.

GCS, on the other hand, operated as a cargo charter operator and received four Boeing 707-330Cs for this purpose in 1977 and 1978. After the old Boeings no longer met the noise and fuel consumption requirements of the early 1980s, GCS replaced them with five McDonnell Douglas DC-8-73CFs. German Cargo Services was renamed

A DC-8-73F of German Cargo Services is towed to its parking position, surrounded by Boeing 747s and 727s and McDonnell Douglas DC-10-30s of its parent company, Lufthansa. *German Cargo Services*

The transport of live animals was a specialty of German Cargo Services. Here a load of cattle is about to be put aboard one of the airline's DC-8s. *German Cargo Services*

Lufthansa Cargo Airlines on May 1, 1993. The last DC-8-73CF with the registration D-ADUE left the Lufthansa Cargo fleet in mid-1997, bringing the sporadic use of the DC-8 as an exotic aircraft in the Lufthansa Group to a definitive end after thirty-two years.

Iberia: Iberia, Compañía Aérea de Transporte, was formally founded on June 28, 1927. During the company's first decade, it linked major cities on the Spanish mainland, the Canary Islands, and North Africa. On May 29, 1961, Iberia took delivery of its first three jet airliners, Douglas DC-8, which it was to use on its long-haul route from Spain to New York, Caracas, San Juan, Mexico City, Havana, and Buenos Aires. Today, Iberia is part of the British-Spanish International Airline Group (IAG), together with British Airways and Aer Lingus.

The career of the Iberia DC-8-52 shown here, with the registration EC-AUM, was relatively uneventful. Delivered to the Spanish national airline on August 28, 1963, it was operated by the company until October 1974, when it was subleased to the airline's charter subsidiary Aviaco. There it was given the name Zurburan. The aircraft was retired in January 1984 and scrapped in March 1987. *Tom Weihe*

Icelandair (see **Loftleidir**)

When photographed by Dirk Grothe at Frankfurt/Main on June 21, 1984, this DC-8-55 with the registration N916R had been leased to Icelandair by Overseas National Airways. Icelandair subsequently purchased the aircraft in January 1986 and operated it for two more years. Its next owner was Kabo Air, which purchased the aircraft in 1988 and converted it into a freighter. This DC-8-55 had originally been delivered to SAS in 1965 with the registration SE-DBD and the name Folke Viking. *Dirk Grothe*

Almost exactly ten years before Dirk Grothe photographed the DC-8-55 N916R in Icelandair colors, Tom Weihe captured it on film at Copenhagen airport. It was then being operated under lease by the Scandinavian airline Scanair. *Tom Weihe*

Inter Swede

This DC-8-51 flew with the short-lived operator Inter Swede from Christmas 1971 to March 1, 1972. It was originally delivered to Trans Caribbean Airways, which gave it the name James Roy in November 1961 after Northwest Orient failed to take delivery of it from Douglas. Other operators were Eastern Air Lines, Cyprus Airways, and the Finnish airline Kar Air. It ended its life at Brussels Airport, where it was scrapped in May 1986. *Tom Weihe*

On March 13, 1974, JAL began operating the DC-8-62 on the route to Copenhagen with the flight number JA8051. *Tom Weihe*

JAL entered the jet age on its long-range routes with the DC-8-32. *JAL / Marcus Kolskog collection*

JAL gave the first-class lounges of its DC-8s a unique look in the Japanese style. *JAL / Marcus Kolskog collection*

Japan Air Lines: The Japanese national airline Japan Air Lines was one of the very early DC-8 customers. Its first aircraft—a DC-8-32 with the registration JA8001 and christened Fuji—was handed over to the airline on July 29, 1960. Further examples of this version followed, with such illustrious names as Nikko, Hakone, and Miyajima. While JAL used the Convair 880 on regional jet routes, it needed four-engine aircraft with the longest possible range for routes to Europe and North America. The first step in this direction was taken with the DC-8-53/54/55, the first of which was taken over on March 27, 1962. The DC-8-62 ultra-long-haul version came at just the right time for JAL, allowing it to fly to Europe with just one refueling stop. For high-volume regional routes at home and abroad, JAL added the Super Sixty DC-8-61 to its DC-8 fleet.

The cockpit of a JAL DC-8 served as a striking background for the airline's route map. *JAL / author's collection*

KLM (see **KSSU**)

The Dutch airline KLM named the DC-8-53 illustrated here after Admiral Richard E. Byrd, the flying polar explorer. The photo was taken at Copenhagen on July 23, 1969. KLM was probably the most faithful Douglas and McDonnell Douglas customer anywhere in the world. Except for the DC-1, it flew every Douglas Commercial type. After the merger of Douglas and McDonnell, it also procured the MD-11, but not the MD-80 or MD-90. *Tom Weihe*

Loftleidir: The airline Loftleidir Icelandic was founded on March 10, 1944, initially for domestic flights on the volcanic island in the North Atlantic. It launched its first international route on June 17, 1947, between the capitals of Iceland and Denmark—Reykjavik and Copenhagen. A Douglas DC-4 was used, followed by the first North American route, to New York, on August 26, 1948. The no-frills fares offered by Loftleidir between Europe and the United States in the 1960s and 1970s became famous. For decades, the airport in the small grand duchy of Luxembourg was the starting point for the connection to New York, flown by four-engine Canadair CL-44 turboprops and DC-8s—with a stopover in Iceland. These low-cost routes attracted a young traveling public in particular, earning Loftleidir the nickname of the "hippie airline" at the end of the 1960s. Among others, the future American president Bill Clinton was an enthusiastic Loftleidir passenger during his student days. In 1973, in the face of a sluggish global economy and increasing competition between airlines on the North Atlantic, the Icelandic government convinced Loftleidir Icelandic and Flugfelag Iceland of the advantages of a merger. The result was Icelandair, which henceforth shed its low-cost image and became a "regular" airline on the North Atlantic. The name "Loftleidir" is by no means history, however, since Icelandair continues to use it occasionally for its wet-lease-and-charter business.

This DC-8-63CF, which Douglas delivered to Seaboard World Airlines on June 21, 1968, had an interesting history. In addition to being leased to Loftleidir of Iceland, it was operated by Air Algerie, Nigeria Airways, Icelandair, Orion Air, and finally as N836UP by United Parcel Service, which in 1984 had the aircraft converted into a DC-8-73CF. *Tom Weihe*

Originally planned for Philippine Airlines, this DC-8-63 was initially delivered to KLM, with the registration PH-DEK and the name David Livingstone. Philippine Airlines leased it from 1972 to 1975 before it returned to service with KLM. The aircraft was acquired by Daedalus Corporation in April 1984. Immediately afterward it was leased by Icelandair, which purchased the DC-8-63 on November 5, 1984, and renamed it Vesturfari. The photo was taken on July 17, 1985, in Luxembourg. By then, Icelandair was already flying the aircraft with the Icelandic registration TF-FLV. *Dirk Grothe*

After it was converted to DC-8-55 standard, Ship One briefly saw service with Lufthansa. This was due to delays in the delivery of Boeing jets. *Lufthansa*

Lufthansa: Although Lufthansa was a loyal Boeing customer, it could not avoid the temporary use of the Douglas DC-8, the Boeing 707's main competitor, on its route network.

The liaison with Boeing's archrival began in 1965, when Lufthansa leased the DC-8 prototype with the construction number 1 from May to December. The German airline leased Ship One, painted in full Lufthansa colors and bearing the American registration N8008D, from the American airline Trans International Airways (TIA) for the 1965 summer season. In December 1960, the jet had already been converted from the original DC-8-11 prototype version, with four Pratt & Whitney JT4 engines, to the DC-8-51 model, with JT3D-1 turbofans and equipped with a passenger cabin. In addition to Lufthansa, the DC-8 prototype was also flown by Aeromexico, Canadian Pacific, and Delta Air Lines until it was retired in 1982. The aircraft was not scrapped until 2001, at the Marana aircraft cemetery in the US state of Arizona.

Lufthansa Cargo (see **German Cargo Services**)

Readying a Lufthansa Cargo DC-8-73F for its next flight at Frankfurt airport. *Lufthansa Cargo*

Pan American World Airways (PAA): The importance of Pan Am to the development of the DC-8 cannot be overstated. Although the hopes for further major Pan Am orders associated with the initial order for twenty-five aircraft on October 13, 1955, were not fulfilled, Douglas might not have continued development of this aircraft type without that order—or even canceled it altogether. In the end, Pan Am received only the brand-new examples of the DC-8-32/33 long-haul version, with the registrations N800PA to N818PA. Pan Am did not take delivery of N819PA and N820PA. Instead, these two aircraft went to its Brazilian subsidiary Panair do Brasil.

DOUGLAS
Service
PAN AMERICAN
THE INTERCONTINENTAL DC-8 JETLINER
JULY-AUGUST 1959

In the summer of 1959, Douglas presented the technical specifications of the first long-range version of the DC-8, using a Pan Am aircraft as an example. *Douglas / Marcus Kolskog collection*

Pan Am DC-8-33s were occasionally used on flights to the United States from the southern German city of Stuttgart, home to such famous companies as Mercedes Benz, Porsche, and Bosch. *Author's collection*

Scandinavian Airlines System (SAS): SAS was founded on August 1, 1946, as a merger of the four largest airlines in Scandinavia: the Norwegian airline DNL, the Danish DDL, and the two Swedish airlines ABA and SILA. In line with the motto "Only together are we strong," the realization that none of the four partner airlines could survive alone in the face of global competition in the long term won out over national egotisms. From 1957, SAS entered the jet age and gradually ordered up to twenty-one of the Sud Aviation S.E. 210 Caravelle in the I, IA, and III versions. The Douglas DC-8-32/33 supplemented the elegant French twin-jet aircraft on long-haul routes from the 1960 summer flight schedule. The first long-haul destinations for the four-engine aircraft were New York and Los Angeles—followed by Tokyo.

SAS operated a total of twenty-eight aircraft from the DC-8 series on its long-haul routes. The seven DC-8-33s, delivered to the Scandinavians from March 31, 1960, were followed by two DC-8-55s in the passenger version and one DC-8-55F freighter. Seven passenger aircraft of the DC-8-62 version, initiated by SAS, one DC-8-62AF all-cargo freighter, and two DC-8-62CFs in the combi version followed. For the first time, they were able to reach the American West Coast nonstop from the SAS hub in Copenhagen. Eight DC-8-63s, including two DC-8-63PFs originally built for Eastern Airlines, rounded off the top end of the SAS DC-8 fleet. The last flight of a DC-8 with an SAS flight number took place on January 22, 1988, marking the end of an almost twenty-eight-year era in the history of this airline.

On May 29, 1966, Tom Weihe photographed the second DC-8-33 delivered to SAS, on May 4, 1960, at Copenhagen airport. It wore the registration LN-MOA and bore the name Haakon Viking. Under SAS management, it was operated for a time by its charter subsidiary Scanair and the then SAS subsidiary company Thai International. *Tom Weihe*

This photo of an SAS DC-8-55 was taken at Copenhagen in April 1969. *Tom Weihe*

SAS DC-8-62 LN-MOW in its 1980s look at Copenhagen against the background of a brilliant blue sky. *Dirk Grothe*

Even after about twenty years of service, at the beginning of the 1980s the airline's DC-8-63s were the background of the SAS long-range fleet, especially on routes to Africa and Asia. *Dirk Grothe*

DC-8-63 OY-KTG in its original livery on April 13, 1974. *Tom Weihe*

Tom Weihe took this photo of SAS DC-8-62 OY-KTE on October 19, 1968. *Tom Weihe*

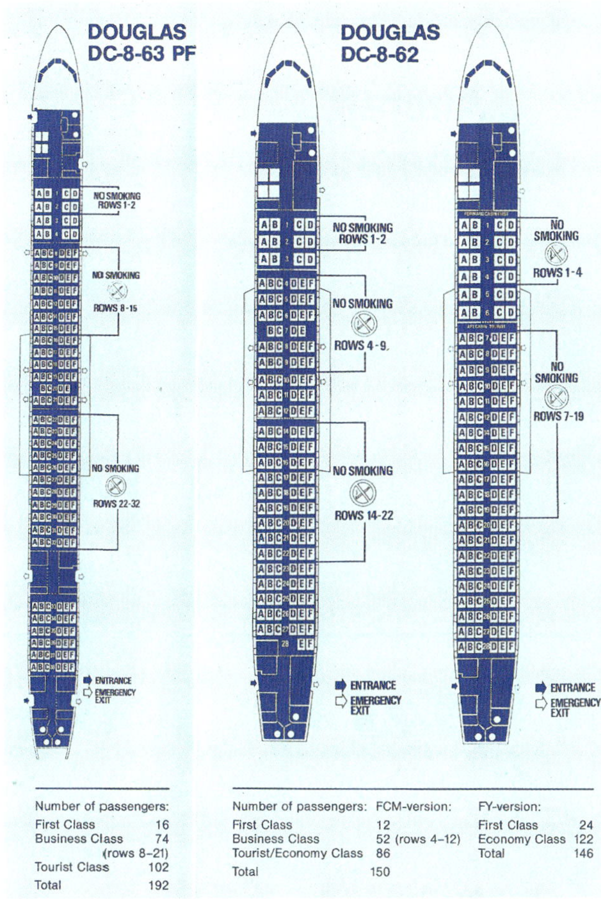

This illustration shows the seating plans of the DC-8 versions operated by SAS in 1984. *SAS / author's collection*

Scanair: The Scandinavian vacation airline Scanair was founded on June 30, 1961, by the three parent companies of SAS. This was in cooperation with the Swedish aircraft manufacturer SAAB, the East Asiatic Company of Denmark, and Skips Marina A/S of Norway. On October 1, 1965, the ownership structure changed and Scanair became a consortium in which only the three owners were involved, in proportion to the 3-2-2 (ABA/DNL/DDL) shares applicable to SAS at the time. Scanair's headquarters were located

Scanair årsredovisning 1985/86.

When Scanair published its 1985–86 business report, the DC-8-63 was the centerpiece of its fleet. *Scanair / author's collection*

All-economy seating on board a Scanair DC-8 Sunjet. *SAS Museum*

Zurich airport was a regular destination for the DC-8F Jet Traders operated by Seaboard World Airlines. *ETH Zurich*

in Stockholm, like those of SAS. Scanair always leased aircraft from SAS and sometimes also from other Scandinavian airlines, such as Boeing 727-100s from Transair Sweden. The DC-8s in the Scanair fleet leased from SAS consisted of the DC-8-55, DC-8-62, and DC-8-63 versions.

The aircraft flew for various northern European tour operators and SAS-owned travel agency chains Globetrotter and Vingresor until they were replaced by Airbus A300s and McDonnell Douglas DC-10-10s. Scanair ceased operations at the end of 1993 after merging with the Danish company Conair to form Premiair.

Seaboard & Western Airlines: The freight and passenger airline Seaboard & Western Airlines was founded by Arthur and Raymond Norden on September 11, 1946. The brothers were veterans of the Second World War and had served in the Army Air Transport Command. At the age of twenty-eight, Raymond became the airline's first president. Arthur, who was four years older, became executive vice president and treasurer.

The name Seaboard & Western can be traced back to the fact that the airline originally operated from the American western seaboard to destinations in western Europe and the Middle East. The airline's first aircraft was a Douglas C-54 that had been sold off by the American military and converted to civil standard. It made its first flight in May 1947, flying a cargo consisting of two horses from Newark to Geneva. The C-54 was followed by Curtiss-Wright C-46s, Douglas DC-3s, Lockheed L-1649D Super Constellations, and Canadair CL-44 "swing tails."

Seaboard & World entered the jet age in June 1964, when it leased a DC-8-55 freighter from Douglas. This version was capable of carrying thirteen cargo pallets with a total payload of 90,000 pounds. At the end of January 1965, Seaboard converted a chartered DC-8-55 into a flying editorial studio and photo lab for *Life* magazine, enabling it to file reports on Winston Churchill's funeral in London.

Seaboard ordered twelve examples of the stretched DC-8-63CF, the first of which was delivered in June 1968. At that time, the DC-8-63 was the largest commercial aircraft in the world.

Seaboard became heavily involved in the Vietnam War, carrying freight into the war zones as well as 138,000 passengers. At least two Seaboard aircraft were hit by enemy gunfire; however, they were able to continue their flights with no injuries or fatalities.

The airline's thirty-three-year history came to an end on October 1, 1980, when it was acquired by Flying Tiger. During that time, the airline was not involved in a single fatal accident.

Spantax: Spanish Air Taxi Líneas Aéreas S.A. was founded on October 6, 1959, by former Iberia pilot Rodolfo Bay Wright and former Iberia cabin attendant Marta Estades Sáez. The airline was originally based at Gran Canaria Airport on the Canary Islands. At the end of 1960 the airline purchased two DC-3s from Swissair, and these were placed into service from May 1961 operating tourist flights within the Canary Islands. Among others, piston-engined types were the Douglas DC-4 and Douglas DC-7. After receiving approval from the Spanish authorities to operate passenger charter flights, the airline moved its headquarters from Gran Canaria to Palma de Mallorca. Spantax was famous for the operation of the four-engined Convair CV 990 Coronado jetliners, and for its many incidents and accidents associated with this type, some of them fatal, questioning the operational safety culture of the airline. Spantax entered the jet age with the CV 990 in February and May 1967. The first samples were purchased secondhand from American Airlines. Between 1968 and 1972, an additional eight Convair 990s would join the fleet, two of which were leased to Iberia between 1967 and 1969 while that airline experienced delays in the delivery of its own Douglas DC-8s. The airline acquired a further four Convairs from Swissair in April, May, and June 1975, and the airline would become the world's largest operator of the type. The last one was retired in the mid-1980s. Spantax purchased two stretched Douglas DC-8-61CFs from Trans Caribbean Airways in February 1973 and would operate an additional four of the type. Due to a fierce competition, Spantax got into financial troubles in 1987 and was sold to the Aviation Finance Group, based in Luxembourg. All restructuring efforts were unsuccessful.

After the Kuwait Investment Authority withdrew from a planned offer to purchase the airline, Spantax ceased all operations on March 29, 1988, leaving some seven thousand passengers stranded around Europe.

The Spanish charter airline Spantax was both famous, mainly on account of its Convair CV 990As, and notorious—for its numerous accidents. It did, however, also operate DC-8-61s, such as aircraft EC-CZE, shown here. It was photographed by Dirk Grothe while on approach to Hamburg airport on August 12, 1981. *Dirk Grothe*

Sterling

This DC-8-63 operated by the Danish charter airline Sterling visited Hanover airport on April 19, 1985. *Dirk Grothe*

Südflug: The second use of a DC-8 by the Lufthansa group, after the DC-8-55 converted from the prototype, took place in 1968, after the merger of the then Lufthansa subsidiary Condor Flugdienst with Südflug, which had been founded in Stuttgart in 1953. Founded by Rul Bückle, from modest beginnings the airline grew from a provider of sightseeing flights over the Baden-Württemberg state capital to a renowned charter operator. Four-engine DC-7Cs initially formed the backbone of the airline, which offered charter flights to the Mediterranean and the Canary Islands on behalf of tour operators. The business did so well that Bückle planned to expand further with a pure jet fleet. He ordered new Douglas DC-9-32 medium-range jets and reached an agreement with Swissair to take over two of its used Douglas DC-8-32 long-range aircraft, which it was replacing with new DC-8-62s. Douglas had difficulties delivering the aircraft, however, and Swissair did not get its new aircraft on time. Consequently, the Swiss retained their DC-8-32s for an entire year longer than planned—and Südflug was forced to look around for expensive replacements, since the planned capacity had already been completely sold to tour operators. The replacement aircraft that were leased in the United States did not live up to the expectations of Bückle or his passengers in terms of cabin equipment, in-flight service, or timeliness. But he had no other choice, since his Südflug airline was not the only one caught up in this unanticipated capacity bottleneck, and there were no better aircraft to be had with which to bridge the waiting period. The high costs associated with the leased aircraft resulted in serious financial losses, which ultimately forced Rul Bückle to give up and sell his airline to the Lufthansa Group. Südflug finally took delivery of the two jet airliners, bearing the German registrations D-ADIR and D-ADIM, on December 23, 1967, and March 15, 1968, but by then it was too late. After the official transfer of the company shares on January 2, 1968, the two jets were operated by Südflug, which had been merged with Condor, until the end of the year, when they were taken over by the German charter airline Atlantis.

The former West German charter airline Südflug was based at Stuttgart airport. Delivery difficulties on the part of Douglas contributed to its early demise—and sale to the Lufthansa Group. *ETH Zurich*

Surinam Airways

Founded in 1955, Surinam Airways is the national airline of Surinam and is based at Paramaribo-Zanderij airport. The DC-8-63 with the registration PH-DEM shown here was delivered to KLM on June 2, 1970, and was named James Cook. Surinam Airways leased it from November 1975 to October 1983. After its sale to African Safari Airways on December 10, 1983, if flew with the registration HB-IBF. *Tom Weihe*

Swissair: The Schweizerische Luftverkehr AG (Swissair) was established on March 26, 1931, following the merger of the Zurich airline Ad Astra-Aero with Balair, based in Basel. During its existence, the airline was characterized by technical competence and its worldwide renowned service. The Swiss airline always prided itself in operating the latest aircraft—such as the Caravelle and the Douglas DC-8. Swissair flew three versions of the Douglas four-engine jet: the DC-8-32, DC-8-53, and DC-8-62.

In 1958, SAS and Swissair entered into a close cooperative agreement. This concerned commercial aspects such as common pool flights, the technical maintenance of the fleet, and operational details.

To achieve better purchase conditions for the acquisition of new equipment by the two relatively small airlines, as of 1958, SAS and Swissair jointly purchased new additions to their fleets in larger numbers. This cooperation first affected the S.E. 210 Caravelle. SAS purchased four aircraft from the manufacturer and initially leased them to Swissair, before they were purchased by the Swiss from their northern European partner. Conversely, Swissair ordered Convair CV 990A Coronado four-engine jet airliners and leased two examples to SAS. The DC-8s operated by SAS and Swissair were also identical in all technical details. SAS assumed responsibility for technical maintenance of the Swissair Caravelles in Sweden. During the DC-8s career with the two airlines, SAS was also responsible for overhauling the Swissair aircraft (see KSSU).

Thai Airways International: In 1959, SAS and the national airline of Thailand, Thai Airways Company Ltd. (TAC), agreed to found Thai Airways International Ltd. (Thai) as a joint venture. TAC had a share of 70 percent, while the remaining 30 percent was held by SAS. As part of this agreement, SAS obligated itself to assume all of Thai International's financial liabilities for the first five years. The plan for the future, divided into five-year segments, envisaged that after the fifth year, SAS and TAC would share the costs equally, while the Thais would subsequently assume full control over Thai Airways International Ltd. But that is not what happened. After the fourth year of cooperation, SAS declared itself ready to support Thai financially until 1968. The original cooperative agreement between TAC and SAS was replaced by a second agreement in 1970, and this lasted until March 1977.

Thai began operation with three DC-6Bs, which it acquired from SAS through lease-purchase, in May 1960. The Scandinavians also sent a large contingent of ground personnel, administration experts, and cockpit crews to Thailand. It proved a very popular change of routine for

A Swissair DC-8-62 over the Swiss Alps. *ETH Zurich*

SAS leased its DC-8-33 SE-DBB Ottar Viking to Thai Airways International from 1970 to 1978. There it was given the registration HS-TGR and the name Suranaree. Thai was then a subsidiary of the Scandinavian airline, and its livery was very reminiscent of that used by the Scandinavian airline. *Tom Weihe*

the SAS employees. SAS also covered all the training expenses for the Thai flight and ground personnel.

The first flights were from Bangkok to Tokyo, but the airline's route network was soon expanded to include the most-important commercial centers in the Far East. The first jet to wear the SAS-Thai company livery was a Convair 990A Coronado leased from SAS in 1962. After initial losses, Thai began showing a profit from the 1964–65 business year and enjoyed a high volume of customers. In 1966, Thai International became the first regional airline in the Far East to operate jet aircraft exclusively. The S.E. 210 Caravelle jet airliners provided by SAS had seventy-two seats. They were joined by two Douglas DC-9-41s in 1970 and five DC-8-33s from SAS in 1970–71. In 1971, Thai opened its first intercontinental route from Bangkok, via Singapore, to the Australian metropolis of Sydney. This route was serviced by DC-8-62s, also leased from SAS. This was followed in 1972 by the first intercontinental route to the main hub of its European shareholder in Copenhagen—followed by London and Frankfurt. By the end of 1973, Thai already had about 2,900 employees and served twenty-one destinations in seventeen countries.

Aircraft that were leased by SAS to Thai for only a short time received this temporary livery with the names of both airlines. *SAS Museum*

SE-DBH Ring Viking was originally delivered to SAS as a new aircraft in 1968. In March 1974 the DC-8-63 was leased to Thai International and sold to the airline on November 1 of that year. In 1968 it returned to the SAS group and henceforth flew for Scanair with its original registration. *Tom Weihe*

In 1975 the Thai government expressed the wish that the ownership of Thai should rest exclusively in the hands of Thais. Consequently, SAS sold its remaining 15 percent share to the Thai government on April 1, 1977. Despite this, the two companies continued their cooperative arrangement in the fields of marketing, sales, operations, technology, and administration until September 30, 1982. This included an SAS chief adviser at Thai headquarters in Bangkok, while SAS pilots continued to fly part of the Thai fleet. The two companies also shared joint sales offices in parts of the globe. By 1987, however, the share of these Scandinavian expats in the Thai staff had been reduced to 1 percent.

In the technical sphere, after adding the Airbus A300B4 to its fleet toward the end of the 1970s, Thai continued to rely on SAS technical knowhow in its maintenance facilities in Stockholm. The Thai jets made the long flight from Thailand to Sweden for major checks. As part of the KSSU agreement, KLM overhauled their engines in Amsterdam, while UTA serviced the APU and undercarriage in Paris.

In 1979, there were two Douglas DC-8-63s and two DC-8-62s flying in the airline's livery. These aircraft and their engines were also overhauled by SAS in its maintenance facilities in Arlanda and Linta. The last DC-8 left the Thai fleet in 1985.

United Airlines: This American airline was involved in development of the DC-8 from the very beginning. Its president, William A "Pat" Patterson, was one of those who advocated designing the cabin cross section of the new airliner to accept six seats per row. It is no surprise, therefore, that United became one of the first customers for the DC-8-11. The airline took delivery of the first aircraft, bearing the registration N8004U and the name Mainliner Capt. R T Freng, on June 3, 1959. It was the eighth DC-8 built, and after its conversion to DC-8-21 standard in March 1964, it flew continuously with United until it was finally retired on January 4, 1978. Boeing finally accepted the Douglas jet in payment and parked it at the Kingman aircraft graveyard until it was scrapped in 1981.

After an extensive training program, United began DC-8 flight operations on September 18, 1959—the same day as Delta Air Lines. Originally founded from the merger of Boeing Air Transport, National Air Transport, Varney Airlines, and Pacific Air Transport in 1931, United Airlines flew the -11, -12, -52, -54F, and -61 versions of the DC-8. Some examples of the last model were converted into DC-8-71s through the adoption of CFM56 turbofan engines. The last flight by a United DC-8-71 took place on October 31, 1991, on the Hawaii–San Francisco route.

Transamerica

Photographer Dirk Grothe captured this DC-8-73CF of the American airline Transamerica as it was taxiing on June 23, 1984. The aircraft was originally built for Overseas National Airways as a DC-8-63CF, in September 1968. It was converted to a DC-8-73 on behalf of United Parcel Service; however, it initially flew for the charter airline Transamerica before it was acquired by the freight airline Flying Tiger. *Dirk Grothe*

By the time this photo was taken, exactly two years had passed since United had had its DC-8-61s converted into DC-8-71s such as the one shown here. *Dirk Grothe*

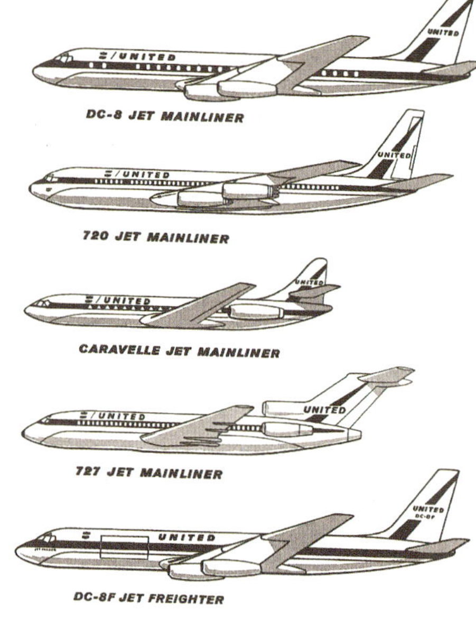

A historical overview of the United fleet of the 1960s. *Marcus Kolskog collection*

Company postcard with the image of a United DC-8-21. *Marcus Kolskog collection*

Company postcard with the image of a DC-8-61. *United / Marcus Kolskog collection*

VIASA

Tom Weihe photographed this DC-8-53 of the Venezuelan airline VIASA at Rome's Fiumicino airport on March 9, 1967. *Tom Weihe*

Worldways

Worldways Canada was a Canadian charter airline that operated from 1973 to 1990. In 1983 it purchased four DC-8-63s from CP Air. One of these was C-FCPP, seen here while visiting an SAS maintenance facility. *Tom Weihe*

THE KSSU QUARTET AND ITS DC-8S: KLM/SAS/SWISSAIR/UTA

IT BEGAN WITH THE DC-8

Decades prior to the now-common alliances in commercial air travel, Swissair and the Scandinavian airline SAS acted together in the selection, definition, and technical maintenance of their fleets. The two airlines began their cooperative efforts with their DC-8-32 long-range jet airliners, seven of which were ordered by SAS and three by Swissair. These aircraft were identical except for the color of the cabin equipment and the external liveries. Since both airlines also operated the S.E. 210 Caravelle and the Convair 990 Coronado, their partnership also extended to these two types. Swissair maintained the CV 990As, while SAS was responsible for the general overhauls of the DC-8s and Caravelles of both airlines. The Dutch airline KLM became an informal partner in the alliance in 1963, initially looking after the Pratt & Whitney JT3 engines of the DC-8-32/33s of all three airlines in Amsterdam. In 1967 it officially became the third partner in the alliance, which was expanded to include the technical work package for the Douglas DC-9, which had been ordered by KLM, SAS, and Swissair.

When the age of the jumbo jet arrived in the late 1960s, SAS, Swissair, and KLM also had to face up to the challenge of operating a combined total of fifteen examples of the Boeing 747 in a commercially sensible way and maintaining them. In 1968 this led to the signing of the KSS (KLM/SAS/Swissair) Agreement, which defined the common technical and operational standards for this type of aircraft and laid down a division of tasks for its overhaul. SAS assumed the task of overhauling the Pratt & Whitney JT9D engines at its facilities in Stockholm Linta, while KLM carried out D-checks on the partners' aircraft in Amsterdam. The APUs of the 747 fleets were serviced by the French company UTA after it joined the alliance in February 1970, creating the KSSU Alliance. A flight simulator operated by KLM in Amsterdam was also used to train KSSU 747 pilots. Initially

This contemporaneous drawing illustrates the cooperation among KLM, SAS, Swissair, and UTA. *ETH Zurich*

created for a period of ten years, the KSSU organization was headed by an eight-person management committee comprising two top managers from each airline. Other working groups concerned themselves with organization cooperation within the KSSU and setting IT standards, as well as legal and financial details. The definition of technical standards and selection of new aircraft types, however, was the job of the Long Term Advisory Group. After rejecting the Lockheed L-1011-84-A, KLM, SAS, and Swissair agreed on the selection of the McDonnell Douglas DC-10. Together they placed an order for fourteen aircraft with options for another twenty-two, becoming the first customers for the -30 long-range version.

Like Lufthansa in the ATLAS alliance, SAS also transferred the largest DC-10 work packages to its partners as part of the KSSU alliance, since it had already taken on an extensive program with the engine overhaul of the joint 747 fleets. KLM in Amsterdam was responsible for the overhaul of the General Electric CF6-50 engines of the KSSU DC-10s, Swissair took over the overhaul of the airframes in Zurich, and UTA provided technical support for the landing gear and the auxiliary power units in the rear for the autonomous power supply of the three-engine aircraft. As a special feature, in addition to its own five DC-10-30s, SAS also brought the fleet of two aircraft of its then subsidiary Thai Airways International into the KSSU alliance. This partnership was extended to include Thai International's Airbus A300B4s in 1978. While SAS carried out a D-check on the aircraft in Stockholm-Arlanda as the largest maintenance event, their General Electric CF6-50 engines were overhauled at KLM in Amsterdam and the auxiliary power units at UTA in Paris.

AN EIGHTY-YEAR DOUGLAS TRADITION

KLM, SAS, and Swissair, three of the most loyal customers of the civil DC (Douglas Commercial) series, were united in the KSSU alliance; these three airlines had operated every commercial aircraft produced by Douglas and McDonnell Douglas (MDC), with the exception of the DC-1. The tradition began with the DC-2 of 1934 and continued to the MD-95, the last passenger jet manufactured at Long Beach before MDC was absorbed by Boeing in 1997.

THE DOUGLAS AIRCRAFT FAMILY IN SERVICE WITH KLM, SAS, UTA, AND SWISSAIR

	DC-1	DC-2	DC-3	DC-4	DC-5	DC-6	DC-7	DC-8	DC-9	DC-10	MD-80	MD-11	MD-90-30	MD-95*
KLM	-	X	X	X	X	X	X	X	X	X		X		
SAS	-		X	X		X	X	X	X	X	X		X	X
SWISSAIR	-	X	X	X		X	X	X	X	X	X	X		
UTA/UAT/TAI			X	X		X	X	X		X				

* SAS subsidiaries BLUE 1 and SPANAIR

CHAPTER 7
THE DC-8'S ROLE IN SCIENTIFIC RESEARCH AND HUMANITARIAN CAUSES

In addition to commercial use, various DC-8s were also used in the humanitarian-aid and scientific-research roles. Here we present three representative organizations: Orbis, NASA, and Samaritan's Purse.

For decades, NASA's DC-8-72 took part in research projects around the world. NASA

ORBIS

For eight years, a DC-8-21 donated by United Air Lines to Project Orbis in 1980 flew around the world on a humanitarian mission. Originally built as a DC-8-11 in 1960, in 1982 the aircraft took to the skies as a flying eye clinic and training center for local ophthalmologists, primarily in Asia and Africa. Initially converted from a DC-8-11 to a DC-8-12—and then upgraded to a DC-8-21 in 1965—the DC-8 named Mainliner Capt. Ralph J. Johnson, with the registration N8038D, flew in regular passenger service for the airline until 1980.

In January 1982 the aircraft began its new life, flying on humanitarian missions with the new registration N220RB. However, the surgical procedures did not take place in flight, but while the aircraft was stationed at the mission location for a longer period of time. The training and eye surgeries were carried out by Project Orbis doctors and medical staff on a voluntary basis. More than 18,000 operations were carried out on board the DC-8-21 during its time as a clinic, and 28,000 doctors and nurses received further training. After it was replaced by a larger DC-10-10 donated by the courier and express service Federal Express and flown by former FedEx pilots, Project Orbis donated its DC-8 to the Chinese aviation museum Datangshan as an exhibit.

The fourth DC-8 built was transformed into a flying eye hospital and a training center for ophthalmologists. It entered service with Orbis in 1982. *Orbis*

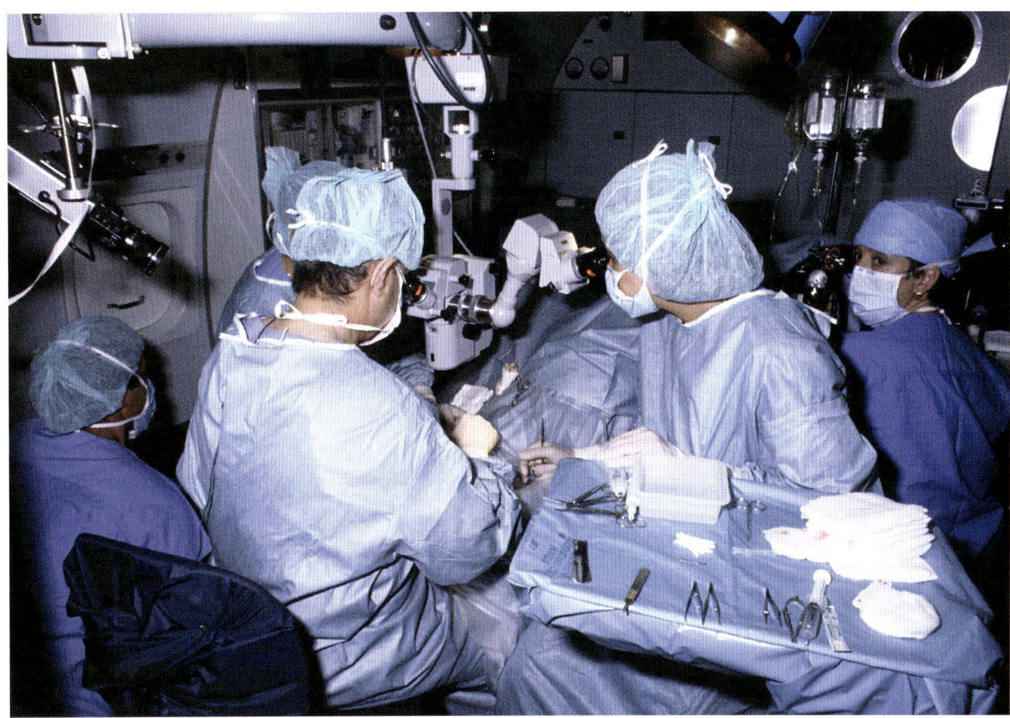

Eye surgery being carried out on board the DC-8-21. *Orbis*

Training doctors and nursing staff in the aircraft cabin. *Orbis*

NASA

On the occasion of its retirement, NASA wrote the following "obituary" for its DC-8-72:

> After 37 years of successful airborne science missions, NASA's DC-8 aircraft completed its final mission and returned to the agency's Armstrong Flight Research Center Building 703 in Palmdale, California, on April 1, 2024.
>
> The DC-8 crew were welcomed back with a celebratory water salute by the US Air Force Plant 42 Fire Department after completing an air quality study, the Airborne and Satellite Investigation of Asian Air Quality, or ASOA-AQ mission. The aircraft was retired in May of that year.
>
> As the largest flying science laboratory in the world, the DC-8 has been used to support the agency's Airborne Science mission since 1987. This unique aircraft was fist acquired by NASA in 1985 and collected data for experiments in support of scientific projects serving the world's scientific community—including scientists, researchers, and students from NASA and other federal, state, academic, and foreign institutions.

At the time of its retirement, it was planned that the DC-8 will continue its educational legacy as it retires to its new home at Idaho State University in Pocatello, Idaho, where it shall be used to train future aircraft technicians by providing real-world experience in the college's Aircraft Maintenance Technology Program.

NASA's DC-8 taking off from Clark International Airport in the Philippines for the flight back to the USA for final decommissioning. *Dirk Grothe*

The NASA DC-8-72 was originally built for the Italian airline Alitalia in 1969. *NASA*

After returning to Palmdale from its final mission, the NASA DC-8 is welcomed back with a celebratory water salute by US Air Force Plant 42 Fire Department. *NASA*

SAMARITAN'S PURSE

The Christian aid organization Samaritan's Purse is globally active wherever people need its help due to natural disasters or famine. It describes itself as follows:

> Samaritan's Purse is a nondenominational evangelical Christian organization providing spiritual and physical aid to hurting people around the world. Since 1970, Samaritan's Purse has helped meet needs of people who are victims of war, poverty, natural disasters, disease, and famine with the purpose of sharing God's love through His Son, Jesus Christ. The organization serves the Church worldwide to promote the Gospel of the Lord Jesus Christ.

Its fleet of aircraft includes a DC-8-72CF, which is the last known example of this aircraft type in use worldwide when this book went to print. Since 1975 the organization has been using aircraft to transport doctors and first responders as well as food, medicine, tents, and other relief supplies to areas affected by emergency situations:

> To support the work of Samaritan's Purse around the world, the aviation arm of Samaritan's Purse operates 24 aircraft, including two helicopters, which are based in strategic locations. The various aircraft are specifically used for ongoing relief and development work in remote areas and are ready to deploy when disasters strike. Samaritan's Purse now operates two cargo planes—a Douglas DC-8 and Boeing 757. These enable Samaritan's Purse to respond at a moment's notice by airlifting tons of emergency relief supplies including Emergency Field Hospitals, shelter material, and water filtration systems anywhere in the world.
>
> - The Samaritan's Purse DC-8 was added to its fleet in 2015. Known as a combi aircraft, it is specially configured to carry up to 74,000 pounds of cargo and 32 passengers, significantly increasing the organization's

capacity to respond immediately in times of crisis around the world.

- Since the organization first deployed it in April of 2016, the DC-8 has carried more than 8.2 million pounds of cargo on 192 missions to locations such as Haiti, Alaska, Mexico, Jamaica, Togo, Colombia, Tanzania, Ethiopia, Italy, and Israel.
- In 2023, the DC-8 carried more than 558,416 pounds of cargo on 11 relief missions.

DC-8 BACKGROUND

Samaritan's Purse purchased the 1968 Douglas DC-8-72CF airplane from an Australian cargo carrier—just before it was going to be turned into scrap parts—to shorten the organization's disaster relief response time as it responds with personnel and supplies all over the world.

Samaritan's Purse inspected, replaced, or refurbished every square inch of the airplane to ensure it met the latest FAA standards.

Less than twenty-four hours after the FAA gave the final sign-off, Samaritan's Purse airlifted an emergency field hospital, doctors, nurses, and disaster response specialists to Ecuador in response to a devastating 7.8 magnitude earthquake. From this location, medical staff treated more than 1,200 people in need.

The DC-8 has a range of 7,000 nautical miles—in perspective, that would be a nonstop flight from Charlotte, North Carolina, to Tokyo.

The aircraft is based at a Samaritan's Purse hangar at Piedmont Triad International Airport in Greensboro, North Carolina.

The DC-8-72F is loaded for its next mission of mercy. *Samaritan's Purse*

CHAPTER 8
THE DC-8 IN THE GOLDEN AGE OF AIR TRAVEL

In the "golden age of air travel," the airplane was still a new means of transport, and air fares were so high that most people around the world could only dream of flying to faraway places.

Air travel was therefore reserved mostly for the "very important people," especially in the 1940s to 1960s, people such as film stars and music legends, representatives of the aristocracy, and industrialists. Even high-ranking politicians were regular guests on board scheduled flights in those days.

With the advent of jet air travel on long-haul routes in the form of the de Havilland Comet, Boeing 707, and Douglas DC-8 at the end of the 1950s and the beginning of the 1960s, the jet set became the epitome of illustrious air travel for wealthy high society. Airlines capitalized on this image and

SAS advertising brochure for its DC-8s. SAS / *author's collection*

Douglas print ad promoting its new jet airliner. *Boeing*

First-class service for the queen of Denmark on board an SAS DC-8-33. *SAS Museum*

advertised their elegant jetliners in global cinema hits such as the James Bond series of films. But it was not just cool British spies who flew on the DC-8, because after the introduction of the cheaper economy travel class on long-haul routes, the aircraft increasingly established itself as a means of transportation for everyone.

PASSENGER BOOM: IN PART THANKS TO THE DC-8

In the years following the end of the Second World War, the number of people traveling between Europe and the United States rose steadily. In the late 1940s, there were around half a million passengers a year, half of whom traveled on ocean liners and half on passenger aircraft, as Pan Am reported in a contemporaneous brochure. Riding the wave of success, and thus emphasizing the international character of its route network, the airline changed its name from Pan American Airways (PAA) to Pan American World Airways (Pan Am) in 1950 and gave itself the slogan "World's Most Experienced Airline." This was no exaggeration, because by the end of the 1950s Pan Am was serving destinations on every continent in the world—with the exception of Antarctica.

SAS used newspaper ads such as this one to promote flights to New York and Los Angeles on its DC-8s. *Author's collection*

It was the first airline in the world to introduce a "corporate design" at the beginning of the jet age, which encompassed not only the aircraft livery but all design aspects of the airline, such as catering items and printed matter, right down to the matchboxes. For many years, its service on board and on the ground was unparalleled by other airlines. A milestone was reached in 1957, however, when for the first time more people crossed the North Atlantic in an airplane than on board an ocean liner. The example of Lufthansa shows the stimulating role played by the beginning of the jet age on the North Atlantic. While the average load factor per flight in 1959, the last year with an all-propeller fleet, was still just over forty passengers, in 1960, the first year of the Boeing 707 jets, this figure jumped to over eighty! Another four years later, the airplane had already impressively overtaken the fast steamers on the North Atlantic, since in 1964 only one in six passengers traveled by ship between Europe and North America.

On October 13, 1955, Pan Am announced the purchase of forty-five US-made jets for a then-record-breaking 269 million US dollars. This included twenty-five DC-8s in the overwater version with Pratt & Whitney JT4 engines and twenty Boeing 707s. This was the first jet order by an American airline for American jet airliners, the largest jet order by a US airline—and the largest order of aircraft, whether jets or propeller-driven aircraft, of all time in terms of value. After Pan Am made its first jet flight over the North Atlantic on October 28, 1958, a few days after a Comet 4 flown by the British airline BOAC (now British Airways), the advantages and disadvantages of jet air transport quickly became apparent. The new jets were twice as big and flew twice as fast as the propeller-driven airliners they replaced—but passenger numbers were initially unable to keep pace with this explosion in service. Airline accountants groaned, and the jets left large gaps in the airlines' balance sheets. And yet—flying by jet was unstoppable. The advantages were too great for travelers, who no longer had to endure rough flights in mountains of clouds on board low-flying propeller airliners.

First-class menu preparation in a DC-8 galley. *SAS Museum*

Official presentation of SAS's first DC-8-33 at Copenhagen-Kastrup airport. *SAS Museum*

GOLDEN DAYS FOR AIRLINES AND CUSTOMERS

But it was not all bad news for the airlines at the beginning of the jet age. After all, the golden age of air travel was not just the glamour that surrounded air travelers. The days when international air fares were set by the International Air Transport Association (IATA) must seem just as golden to today's airline managers. And not just the fares. IATA airlines also regulated such important service details as the minimum distance between rows of seats in first, tourist and economy classes. It was also specified what food and drinks could be offered free of charge in the individual classes and whether films could be shown during certain flights.

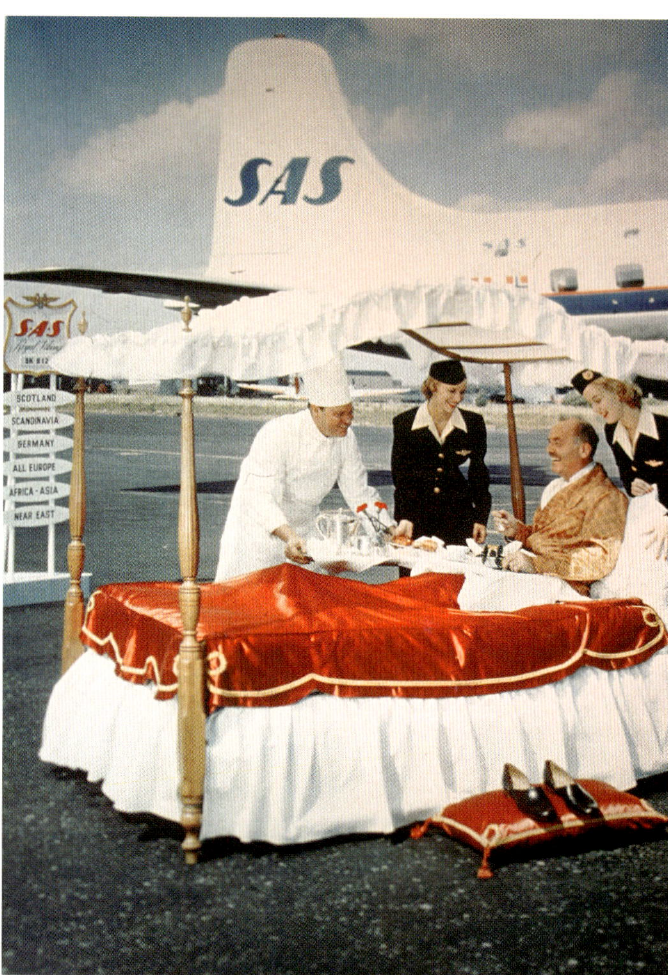

Not a DC-8, but this photo with a DC-7 in the background illustrates the status of airline passengers at that time. *SAS Museum*

Although this is a posed press photo, the DC-8's passengers in fact were provided with red carpets. *SAS Museum*

WHEN YOU FLY DELTA ROYAL JET SERVICE...YOU

You can expect *Royal Jet Service* whether you have a deluxe first class ticket, or one for the thrifty supercoach. Each is the finest of its kind. Each is *Royal Jet* service.

Passengers in the deluxe section enjoy more spacious surroundings and numerous extras that make the trip memorable.

Supercoach passengers get there just as fast ...ride in accommodations far more luxurious and comfortable than first class of a few years ago. And they save about 25%.

No "walking" chessmen in this vibration-free lounge in the deluxe section of the DC-8

Luncheon or dinner is the high point of Delta Royal Jet Service.

A fine champagne sparkles in your glass — heralding the beginning of an incomparable Delta luncheon or dinner, featuring your choice of entrée. All *compliments de la maison*.

The quality of Delta's cuisine matches the excellence of Delta's flight equipment. A truly fine champagne is served. A variety of other popular beverages and cocktails are available in flight. A fresh and modern design of service-ware gives your food tray a gay flair when it is served.

Catering to varied tastes, Delta offers a choice of entrée. A prime and properly aged filet, charcoal broiled to order. Cornish Game Hen, done to a succulent, delicate turn. Or perhaps Lobster Thermidor, if you prefer, on appropriate days. A meal fit to put before a king.

DELTA'S THRIFTY SUPERCOACH

As the Colonial apostle of thrift and efficiency, Benjamin Franklin would have applauded Delta's thrifty supercoach.

Compared to a coach-and-four's speed of perhaps 40 miles a day, the DC-8's speed of nearly 600 miles an hour would be a pleasant, although difficult-to-believe, improvement, even to Franklin's scientific mind . . . especially while enjoying a complimentary repast such as few taverns of the day could boast, in luxury unknown to the times.

Most appealing to Poor Richard's author, however, would be the fare — reasonable in the extreme—*only about five pennies a mile*, roughly comparable to the stagecoach fare between Philadelphia and Baltimore.

BENJAMIN FRANKLIN, 1706-1790.
Patriot, statesman, inventor, author.
"A penny saved is a penny earned."

DELTA DC-8

Built by Douglas, this is the world's most advanced type of jetliner. Of fifteen cities in the U.S. now, or soon to be, on jetliner schedules, Delta will serve seven. Other cities will be added to the jet service pattern as additional equipment is delivered.

New York. . . . PLaza 1-6600
Detroit. WOodward 5-3000
Miami. . . . . FRanklin 3-0441
Houston . . . . CApitol 5-1361
Dallas. . . FLeetwood 7-6161
Atlanta . . . . JAckson 4-3242
Chicago. . . FInancial 6-5300

FIRST CLASS ON DELTA

You'll marvel, as you enter the deluxe cabin, at how such a large, spacious room, handsomely decorated in rich panelling and hand-loomed fabrics, could possibly zip through the air at nearly 10 miles a minute . . . with such incredible smoothness.

Delta Air Lines proudly presented its new DC-8s in this advertising brochure. *Delta Air Lines*

First-class service for passengers sitting in the Palomar seats designed for the DC-8. *SAS Museum*

The "stateroom" on board a DC-8-33. *SAS Museum*

In order to fill the planes, and thus their coffers, the airlines did not have to undercut each other on price as they do today—on the contrary, they had to outdo each other in terms of service to their customers! Half a century ago, what is now known as "advertising and sales promotion" was an indispensable tool for the economic success of an airline.

With flowery words and beautiful pictures, the airlines wooed potential passengers for a flight in a supposedly more comfortable seat, with a more sumptuous onboard menu, served by friendlier staff, and—particularly important at the time—with a more extensive selection of spirits on the long overseas flights.

As a result, large budgets were used by the airlines to woo customers. City offices of the leading airlines in the world's major cities enticed passersby to take a flight to distant lands. The displays often included large models of their jet airliners, in which the interior was reproduced in detail—thus giving an impression of the future flying experience. To this day, such large models of the Douglas DC-8 in the colors of Air Canada, Pan Am, or SAS are coveted collector's items.

The airlines engaged the best designers from their respective nations, to create not only the best possible showcases for the world on the ground, but also the exterior and interior appearance of their aircraft. Special tableware and cutlery as well as aircraft seats were developed not only for the different service classes, but even for individual aircraft types.

The design by architects Edward Larabee Barnes and Charles Forberg for Pan American World Airways, which was implemented on the Douglas DC-8 and other aircraft, was trendsetting. They not only gave the airline's aircraft a new look but also consistently implemented their design ideas in all aspects of the airline visible to the public. This started with advertising material, through to the design of airline offices, catering articles, and the appearance of the aircraft cabins, which they redesigned together with textile designer Jack Lenor. This commission, awarded in 1955, is regarded as the birth of modern corporate design, which at that time was the first holistic design approach to be implemented in the aviation industry.

The Scandinavian airline SAS also commissioned famous Scandinavian designers to come up with a design for the cabin of its DC-8 jets, especially the "stateroom" in the front part of the first-class cabin. This was a feature offered by Douglas that was popular with almost all early DC-8 customers. It allowed four premium passengers, two

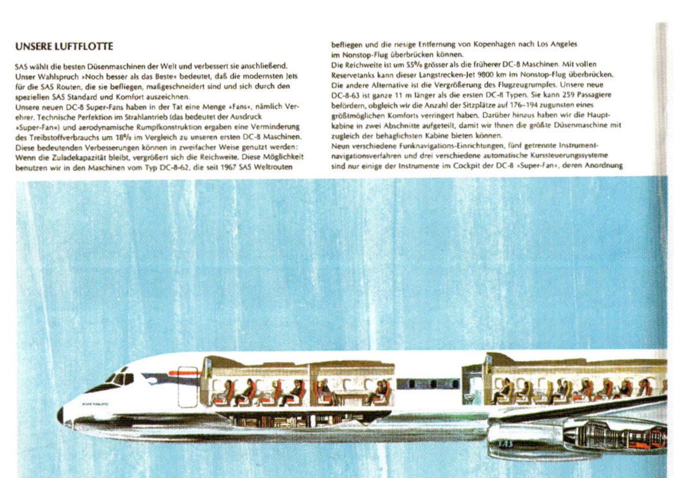

UNSERE LUFTFLOTTE

SAS wählt die besten Düsenmaschinen der Welt und verbessert sie anschließend. Unser Wahlspruch »Noch besser als das Beste« bedeutet, daß die modernsten Jets für die SAS Routen, die sie befliegen, maßgeschneidert sind und sich durch den speziellen SAS Standard und Komfort auszeichnen.

Unsere neuen DC-8 Super-Fans haben in der Tat eine Menge »Fans«, nämlich Verehrer. Technische Perfektion im Strahlantrieb (das bedeutet der Ausdruck »Super-Fan«) und aerodynamische Rumpfkonstruktion ergaben eine Verminderung des Treibstoffverbrauchs um 18% im Vergleich zu unseren ersten DC-8 Maschinen.

Diese bedeutenden Verbesserungen können in zweifacher Weise genutzt werden: Wenn die Zuladekapazität bleibt, vergrößert sich die Reichweite. Diese Möglichkeit benutzen wir in den Maschinen vom Typ DC-8-62, die seit 1967 SAS Weltrouten befliegen und die riesige Entfernung von Kopenhagen nach Los Angeles im Nonstop-Flug überbrücken können.

Die Reichweite ist um 55% grösser als die früherer DC-8 Maschinen. Mit vollen Reservetanks kann dieser Langstrecken-Jet 9800 km im Nonstop-Flug überbrücken.

Die andere Alternative ist die Vergrößerung des Flugzeugrumpfes. Unsere neue DC-8-63 ist ganze 11 m länger als die ersten DC-8 Typen. Sie kann 259 Passagiere befördern, obgleich wir die Anzahl der Sitzplätze auf 176–194 zugunsten eines größtmöglichen Komforts verringert haben. Darüber hinaus haben wir die Hauptkabine in zwei Abschnitte aufgeteilt, damit wir Ihnen die größte Düsenmaschine mit zugleich der behaglichsten Kabine bieten können.

Neun verschiedene Funknavigations-Einrichtungen, fünf getrennte Instrumentnavigationsverfahren und drei verschiedene automatische Kurssteuerungssysteme sind nur einige der Instrumente im Cockpit der DC-8 »Super-Fan«, deren Anordnung

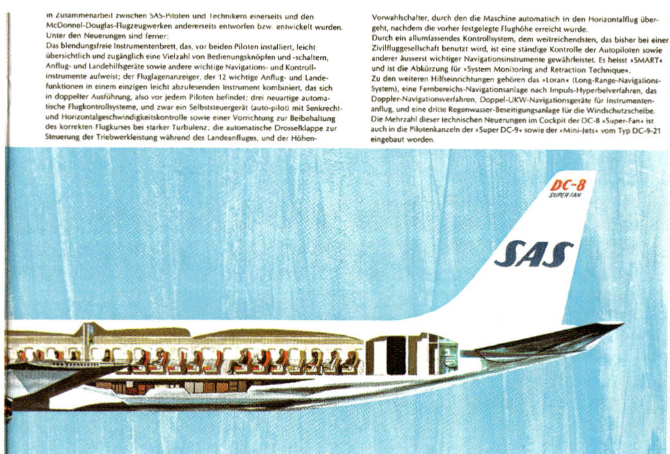

in Zusammenarbeit zwischen SAS-Piloten und Technikern einerseits und den McDonnel-Douglas-Flugzeugwerken andererseits entworfen bzw. entwickelt wurden.

Unter den Neuerungen sind ferner:

Das blendungsfreie Instrumentenbrett, das, vor beiden Piloten installiert, leicht übersichtlich und zugänglich eine Vielzahl von Bedienungsknöpfen und -schaltern, Anflug- und Landehilfsgeräte sowie andere wichtige Navigations- und Kontrollinstrumente aufweist; der Fluglagenanzeiger, der 12 wichtige Anflug- und Landefunktionen in einem einzigen leicht abzulesenden Instrument kombiniert, das sich in doppelter Ausführung, also vor jedem Piloten befindet; drei neuartige automatische Flugkontrollsysteme, und zwar ein Selbststeuergerät (auto-pilot) mit Senkrecht- und Horizontalgeschwindigkeitskontrolle sowie einer Vorrichtung zur Beibehaltung des korrekten Flugkurses bei starker Turbulenz; die automatische Drosselklappe zur Steuerung der Triebwerkleistung während des Landeanfluges, und der Höhenvorwahlschalter, durch den die Maschine automatisch in den Horizontalflug übergeht, nachdem die vorher festgelegte Flughöhe erreicht wurde.

Durch ein allumfassendes Kontrollsystem, dem weitreichendsten, das bisher bei einer Zivilfluggesellschaft benutzt wird, ist eine ständige Kontrolle der Autopiloten sowie anderer äusserst wichtiger Navigationsinstrumente gewährleistet. Es heisst »SMART« und ist die Abkürzung für »System Monitoring and Retraction Technique«.

Zu den weiteren Hilfseinrichtungen gehören das »Loran« (Long-Range-Navigations-System), eine Fernbereichs-Navigationsanlage nach Impuls-Hyperbelverfahren, das Doppler-Navigationsverfahren, Doppel-UKW-Navigationsgeräte für Instrumentenanflug, und eine dritte Regenwasser-Beseitigungsanlage für die Windschutzscheibe.

Die Mehrzahl dieser technischen Neuerungen im Cockpit der DC-8 »Super-Fan« ist auch in die Pilotenkanzeln der »Super DC-9« sowie der »Mini-Jets« vom Typ DC-9-21 eingebaut worden.

Graphic representation of the cabin of an SAS DC-8-63 in the early 1970s. *SAS / author's collection*

seated facing the direction of flight and two facing the opposite direction, to enjoy the flight together at a table in a particularly intimate area separated from the rest of the first-class cabin.

CATHEDRALS OF THE JET AGE

Pan Am and TWA built spectacular terminals at New York's Idlewild Airport, now John F. Kennedy, where their guests received exclusive service. Designed by world-famous architects, the TWA Flight Center and the Pan Am Worldport were impressive steel-and-concrete cathedrals of progress. Many aviation enthusiasts still mourn the demolition of the former Pan Am Terminal at JFK, but at least the Saarinen Terminal has been preserved for posterity. Today it is the reception hall of a hotel built around it, which was designed entirely in the spirit of TWA and Howard Hughes.

Europe was also gearing up for the jet age; for example, with the construction of a jet gateway terminal in Copenhagen. One year after the first scheduled flight by an SAS S.E. 210 Caravelle and at the same time as the delivery of the first Scandinavian Douglas DC-8-32/33 long-haul jets, Copenhagen Airport entered the dawning jet age with a terminal that was considered futuristic at the time. The airport in the Danish capital is traditionally the largest SAS hub and was the starting point for all long-haul routes of this type at the dawn of the DC-8 era.

When today's CPH Terminal 2 was opened by King Frederik of Denmark on April 30, 1960, a row of stores, showers, and a hotel in the transit area offered all the travel comforts that are taken for granted today but were still a sensation at the time. For the first time, passengers in Copenhagen were able to reach their aircraft via a jet bridge system without getting wet, which was still an absolute rarity, at least in Europe. As an anecdote, it should be noted

A WORLDWIDE WELCOME

From Abadan to Amsterdam, Bangkok to Buenos Aires, Nairobi to New York – airports across 5 continents host the SAS traveler. Perfect example of this is the ultra-modern airport at Copenhagen – Europe's gayest gateway. Opened summer, 1960, Copenhagen Airport – 1,680 acres in area – is the smooth-running hub of SAS worldwide operations. In 1964, three million passengers used this airport-metropolis, and approximately 50,000 tons of freight passed through here.

But statistics aside, it is the warm, bright Terminal Building that really holds the welcome. For mothers traveling with children, there are the kiddie-carts and comprehensively equipped nurseries. Modernity prevails in the restaurants – ladies' make-up room – special VIP rooms reservable for press interviews, meetings, etc. – and an elegant foyer, unbelievably cozy in spite of its huge dimensions, where passengers can relax in comfort. Here, too, visitors can purchase duty-free tobacco and liquor, browse last-minute for high-quality Scandinavian Modern treasures, and buy first-class Danish farm produce, the world's newspapers, cosmetics, jewelry and toys.

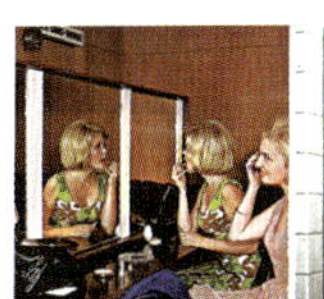

Time off for a new face? . . . Adjoining the ladies' washroom is a special make-up room complete with vanity-table.
In the gentlemen's washroom, plugs are available for use of electric shavers.

Should you arrive travel-weary, shower and bath facilities are available for as little as 50 cents or 4 shillings. In addition, a limited number of separate rest cabins can be rented: charge US $1.50 or 10 shillings each.

Children's playpens and cribs can be set up at various points around the passenger lounge or in the individual nurseries. Each nursery is also equipped with toilet, sink – and a couch, in case mother wants a nap, too.

The Tax-free Gateway Store offers a large and varied selection of the world's leading brands of whisky, champagne and other liquors. Cigarettes, cigars and tobacco may also be bought here at duty-free prices.

The airport's closed-circuit television screens announce – and show – your flight departure. Here you'll also see the gate number from which your aircraft departs and if your flight has already been called, the screen will indicate this.

Wonderful Copenhagen - the hub of SAS world travel

Graphic representation of Copenhagen-Kastrup airport after its expansion to accommodate jet traffic. SAS / *author's collection*

Meticulous checks are made in the soundproof engine control room adjoining each test cell.

Weight distribution to a hairsbreadth. Modern apparatus ensures the dynamic balance of rotors in all gyro instruments.

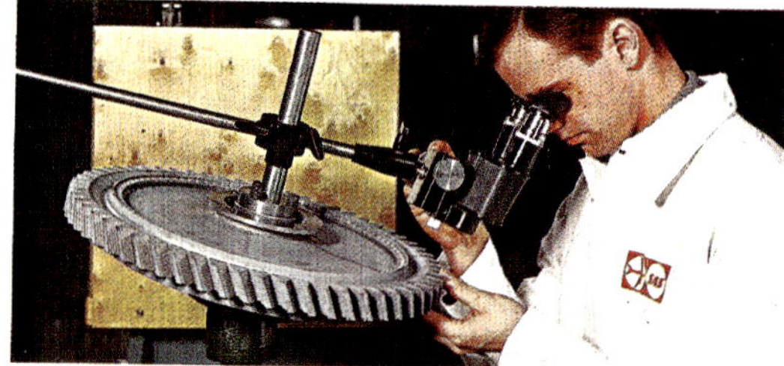

The fir-tree serrations in an Avon turbine wheel come in for close inspection.

Servicing the engines of the DC-8-33, as seen by a contemporary advertisement artist. *SAS / author's collection*

that these bridges were not allowed to be wider than the platforms at the railroad stations, at the insistence of the Danish state railroad, so as not to give air traffic an additional competitive advantage. Fortunately, the jets did not have to fly as slowly as the trains traveled! However, the boom in air traffic was unstoppable, and just nine years later the handling facilities had to be extended to include a domestic and arrivals terminal as well as the third bridge complex for docking the first jumbo jets. This basic layout of Copenhagen Airport, which has been repeatedly expanded and modernized, has remained unchanged to this day, and the six passenger piers have also met generous international standards for many years—without the approval of the railroads.

Douglas DC-8-55

Langdistansefly med turbofan-motorer og forlenget rekkevidde.
Produsent: Douglas, USA

Registreringsmerker og navn

LN-MOH	Harald Viking
OY-KTC	Gorm Viking
SE-DBD	Folke Viking

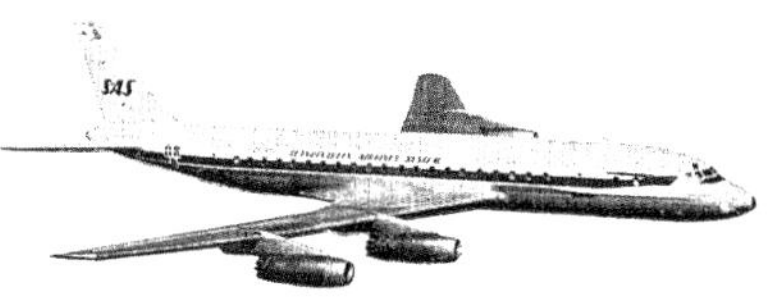

Data

Antall passasjerer	Første klasse	16
	Økonomi/turistklasse	129
	Totalt	145
Fraktvolum	38,7 m³	
Bruttovekt	147 400 kg	
Maksimal last	19 000 kg	
Total lengde	45,9 m	
Vingespenn	43,4 m	
Maks. hastighet	950 km/t (Mach 0.88)	
Marsjfart	875 km/t (Mach 0.81)	
Maks. høyde	13 000 m	
Marsjhøyde	10 000 m	
Aksjonsradius	8 400 km	
Brenseltanker	90 000 l	
Forbruk pr. time	6 800 l	
Motorer	Pratt & Whitney JT3D-3B	
Total starteffekt	32 600 kg	

8

Douglas DC-8-33

Langdistansefly. Produsent: Douglas, USA

Registreringsmerker og navn

LN-MOA	Haakon Viking
LN-MOT	Olav Viking
OY-KTA	Dan Viking
OY-KTB	Bue Viking
SE-DBA	Rurik Viking
SE-DBB	Ottar Viking
SE-DBC	Visbur Viking

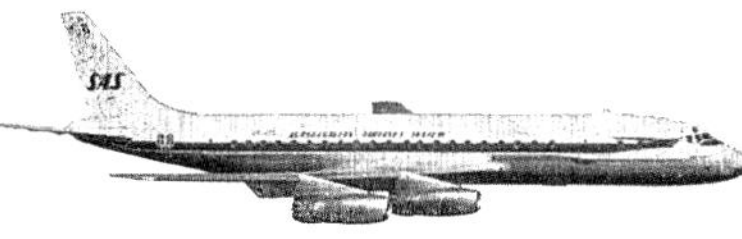

Data

Antall passasjerer	Første klasse	16
	Økonomi/turistklasse	122
	Totalt	138
Fraktvolum	38,7 m³	
Bruttovekt	142 900 kg	
Maksimal last	19 000 kg	
Total lengde	45,9 m	
Vingespenn	43,4 m	
Maks. hastighet	950 km/t (Mach 0.88)	
Marsjfart	875 km/t (Mach 0.81)	
Maks. høyde	13 000 m	
Marsjhøyde	10 000 m	
Aksjonsradius	6 500 km	
Brenseltanker	83 000 l	
Forbruk pr. time	8 500 l	
Motorer	Pratt & Whitney JT4A-9	
Total starteffekt	30 400 kg	

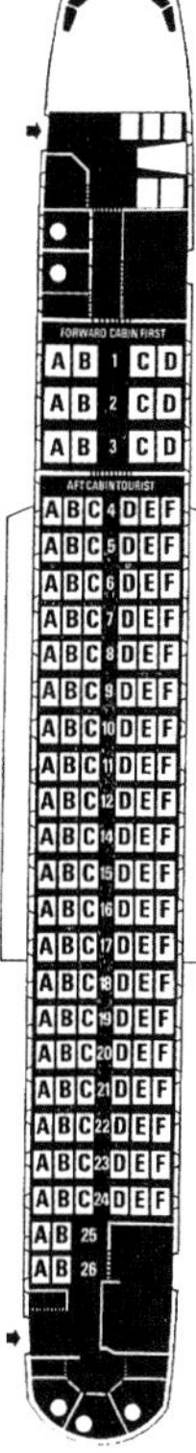

9

The seating plans of the SAS DC-8 fleet in 1968. *SAS / author's collection*

Douglas DC-8 Super 62

Langdistansefly. Produsent: Douglas, USA

Registreringsmerker og navn

LN-MOO	Sverre Viking
OY-KTD	Knud Viking
SE-DBE	Anund Viking
SE-DBF	Ingvar Viking
SE-DBG	Jorund Viking

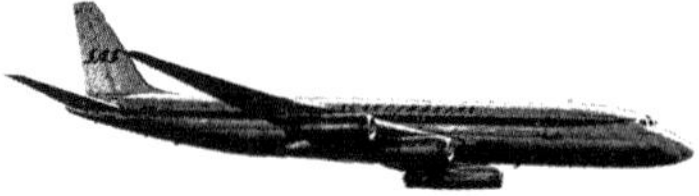

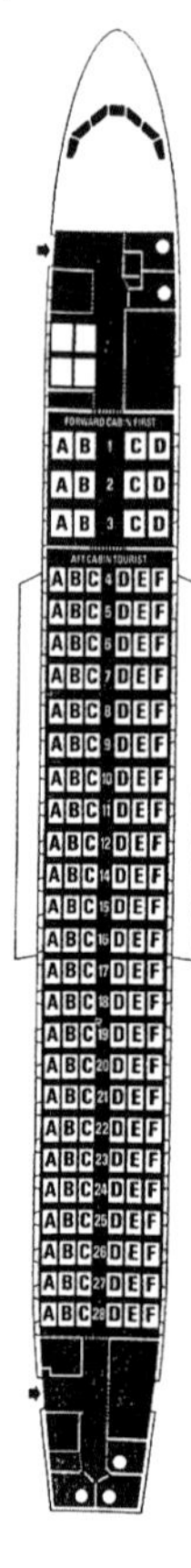

Data

Antall passasjerer	Første klasse	12
	Økonomi/turistklasse	144
	Totalt	156
Fraktvolum	44,8 m³	
Bruttovekt	152 000 kg	
Maksimal last	22 500 kg	
Total lengde	47,9 m	
Vingespenn	45,2 m	
Maks. hastighet	950 km/t (Mach 0.88)	
Marsjfart	875 km/t (Mach 0.81)	
Maks. høyde	13 000 m	
Marsjhøyde	10 000 m	
Aksjonsradius	9 800 km	
Brenseltanker	92 000 l	
Forbruk pr. time	6 600 l	
Motorer	Pratt & Whitney JT3D-3B	
Total starteffekt	32 600 kg	

7

Douglas DC-8 Super 63

Langdistansefly. Produsent: Douglas, USA

Registreringsmerker og navn

LN-MOU	Leif Viking
LN-MOY	Eirik Viking
OY-KTF	Frode Viking
SE-DBH	Ring Viking

Data

Antall passasjerer	Første klasse	16– 16
	Økonomi/turistkl.	178–160
	Totalt	194–176*)
Fraktvolum	70,0 m³	
Bruttovekt	161 000 kg	
Maksimal last	30 000 kg	
Total lengde	57,1 m	
Vingespenn	45,2 m	
Maks. hastighet	950 km/t (Mach 0.88)	
Marsjfart	875 km/t (Mach 0.81)	
Maks. høyde	13 000 m	
Marsjhøyde	10 000 m	
Rekkevidde	8 300 km	
Brenseltanker	92 000 l	
Forbruk pr. time	7 600 l	
Motorer	Pratt & Whitney JT3D-7	
Total starteffekt	34 400 kg	

*) Vinterversjon.

7

CHAPTER 9
TECHNICAL DETAILS

DC-8 PERFORMANCE

Per *Douglas Service Bulletin*, May–June 1959

Figures below are for a block distance of 2,000 nau-tical miles.

Payload: 35,680 lbs.
Takeoff weight: 244,500 lbs.
Takeoff field length (sea level): 5,910 ft.
Landing weight: 183,800 lbs.
Landing-field length (sea level): 6,400 ft.
Block speed: 459 knots
Cruise speed: 494 knots
Fuel burned: 60,700 lbs.
Cruise altitude: 30,000 ft.
Average rate of climb to cruise altitude: 1,980 ft./min.
All-engine takeoff rate of climb at sea level: 2,150 ft./min.
Maximum takeoff weight: 287,500 lbs.
Maximum landing weight: 194,000 lbs.
Maximum zero-fuel weight: 170,550 lbs.
Operating empty weight: 130,804 lbs.
Number of passengers (mixed first class and tourist): 132
Cargo volume: 1,390 ft.[3]

Figures below are for a block distance of 4,970 nautical miles.

Payload: 26,500 lbs.
Takeoff weight: 310,000 lbs.
Takeoff field length (sea level): 9,220 ft.
Landing weight: 175,900 lbs.
Landing-field length (sea level): 6,090 ft.
Block speed: 457 knots
Cruise speed: 478 knots
Fuel burned: 134,100 lbs.
Cruise altitude: variable
Average rate of climb to cruise altitude: 1,245 ft./min.
All-engine takeoff rate of climb at sea level: 1,750 ft./min.
Maximum takeoff weight: 310,000 lbs.
Maximum landing weight: 199,500 lbs.
Maximum zero-fuel weight: 176,500 lbs.

Operating empty weight: 132,234 lbs.
Number of passengers (mixed first class and tourist): 132
Cargo volume: 1,390 ft.[3]

EARLY DC-8 CONFIGURATIONS

From the outset, the DC-8 was offered with three different engine types: the Pratt & Whitney JT3C-6 and JT4A-3 and the Rolls-Royce Conway—the first turbofan engine in the world for passenger jets. Even in the summer of 1959, the technical details of the British engine were still closely guarded secrets, so revolutionary was the design of this first engine with a fan positioned in front of the engine core. Not only is the turbofan engine less noisy, but it also produces additional thrust, although the amount of added thrust was minimal in the early turbofan engines.

Putting the finishing touches on the first SAS DC-8-33, OY-KTA Dan Viking, out of doors on the ramp of the Douglas factory in Long Beach. *SAS Museum*

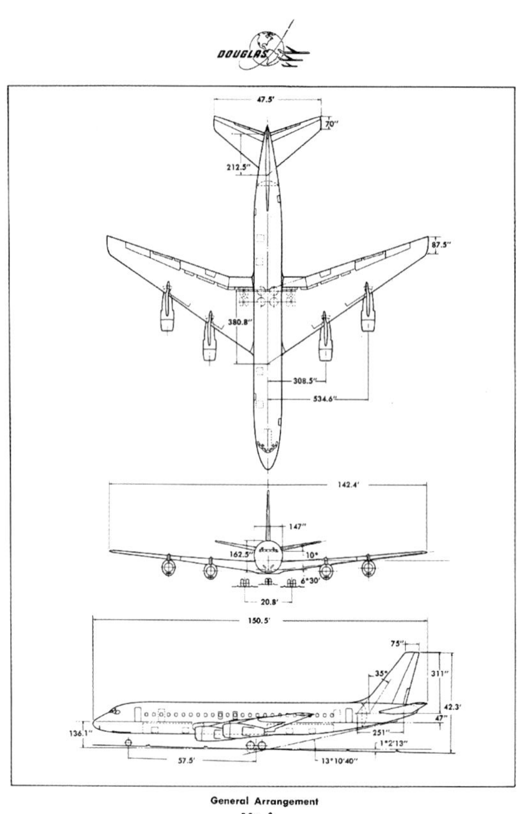

This illustration shows the shape and dimensions of a Douglas DC-8-50. *Boeing*

Engine: Pratt & Whitney JT3C
Maximum takeoff weight: 265,000 lbs.
Maximum landing weight: 189,000 lbs.
Fuel capacity: 17,600 gallons
Number of tanks: 8

Engine: Pratt & Whitney JT4A & Rolls-Royce Conway
Maximum takeoff weight: 265,000 lbs.
Maximum landing weight: 189,000 lbs.
Fuel capacity: 17,600 gallons
Number of tanks: 8

Engine: Pratt & Whitney JT4A & Rolls-Royce Conway
Maximum takeoff weight: 287,500 lbs.
Maximum landing weight: 194,000 lbs.
Fuel capacity: 21,620 gallons
Number of tanks: 9

Engine: Pratt & Whitney JT4A & Rolls-Royce Conway
Maximum takeoff weight: 310,000 lbs.
Maximum landing weight: 199,500 lbs.
Fuel capacity: 21,920 gallons
Number of tanks: 9

Engine: Pratt & Whitney JT4A & Rolls-Royce Conway
Maximum takeoff weight: 310,000 lbs.
Maximum landing weight: 199,500 lbs.
Fuel capacity: 23,300 gallons
Number of tanks: 10

While there was little difference in the external appearance of the early versions of the DC-8, apart from their engine pods, they did differ considerably in the number of fuel tanks and thus in weight and range. A good example of this is provided by the seven DC-8-33s operated by SAS, which were delivered from Douglas with maximum fuel loads of 66,950 kg, 85,075 kg, and 71,080 kg (147,600, 187,558, and 156,700 lbs.).

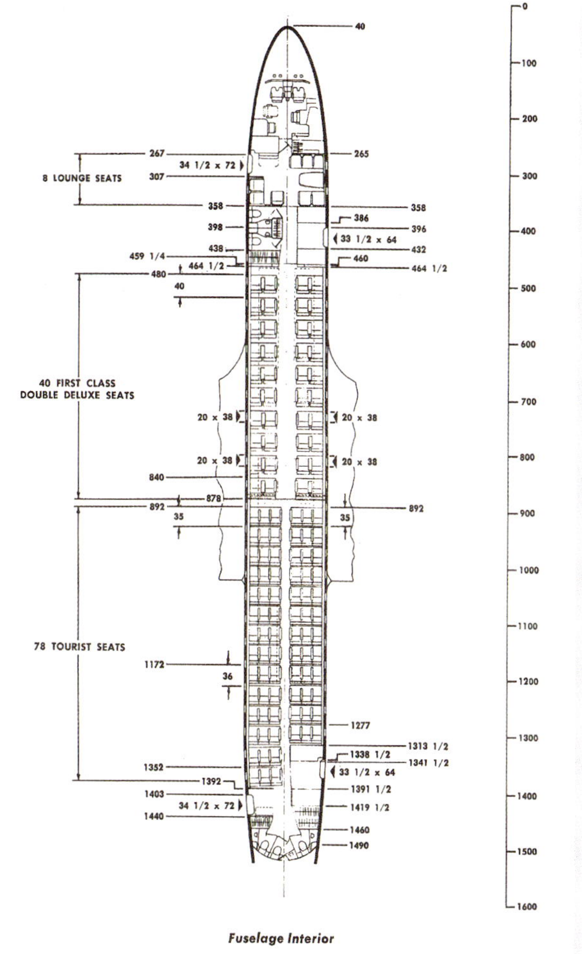

The cabin layout proposed by Douglas for the early versions of the DC-8 was accepted by most airlines with no major changes. *Boeing*

THE DOUGLAS DC-8 SUPER SIXTIES

Maximum seating capacity with 34-inch pitch:
DC-8-62: 189 passengers
DC-8-61 & 63: 251 passengers
(in each case the exit limit)
DC-8-62: Fuselage stretched by 80 inches over the basic DC-8 versions.
DC-8-61 & 63: Fuselage stretch by 440 inches over basic DC-8 versions.

The DC-8-11 on its maiden flight. *Boeing*

GENERAL ARRANGEMENT, DC-8-61

Design weights in pounds:
Operator's weight empty: 148,897
Payload (weight limited): 75,103
Maximum ramp weight: 328,000
Maximum takeoff weight: 325,000
Maximum landing weight: 240,000
Maximum zero-fuel weight: 224,000
Capacity fuel (pounds): 156,733
Capacity fuel (US gallons): 23,393

GENERAL ARRANGEMENT, DC-8-61F

Design weights in pounds:
Operator's weight empty: 142,750
Payload (weight limited): 91,250
Maximum ramp weight: 328,000
Maximum takeoff weight: 325,000
Maximum landing weight: 250,000
Maximum zero-fuel weight: 234,000
Capacity fuel (pounds): 156,733
Capacity fuel (US gallons): 23,393

GENERAL ARRANGEMENT, DC-8-62

Design weights in pounds:
Operator's weight empty: 141,903
Payload (weight limited): 53,097
Maximum ramp weight: 338,000
Maximum takeoff weight: 335,000
Maximum landing weight: 240,000
Maximum zero fuel weight: 195,000
Capacity fuel (pounds): 162,576
Capacity fuel (US gallons): 24,265

GENERAL ARRANGEMENT, DC-8-62F

Design weights in pounds:
Operator's weight empty: 133,246
Payload (weight limited): 96,754
Maximum ramp weight: 338,000
Maximum takeoff weight: 335,000
Maximum landing weight: 250,000
Maximum zero-fuel weight: 230,000
Capacity fuel (pounds): 162,576
Capacity fuel (US gallons): 24,265

GENERAL ARRANGEMENT, DC-8-63

Design weights in pounds:
Operator's weight empty: 155,349
Payload (weight limited): 66,665
Maximum ramp weight: 353,000
Maximum takeoff weight: 350,000
Maximum landing weight: 245,000
Maximum zero-fuel weight: 224,000
Capacity fuel (pounds): 162,576
Capacity fuel (US gallons): 24,265

GENERAL ARRANGEMENT, DC-8-63F

Design weights in pounds:
Operator's weight empty: 146,386
Payload (weight limited): 91,614
Maximum ramp weight: 353,000
Maximum takeoff weight: 350,000
Maximum landing weight: 254,000
Maximum zero-fuel weight: 238,000
Capacity fuel (pounds): 162,576
Capacity fuel (US gallons): 24,265

IMPROVED DESIGN FEATURES OF THE 60 SERIES

Increased wingspan

Wing tips of the Model 62 and 63 series have been extended 3 feet on each side. The resulting increase in square footage of the wing area has expanded the fuel capacity by 72 gallons on each side. Revised leading-edge tanks provide an additional fuel capacity of 340 gallons on each side.

Cutback pylon and long-duct engine pods

The Model 62 and 63 series incorporate aerodynamic improvements such as the cutback engine pylon, which joins the underside of the wing 5 percent aft of the leading edge.

A D-check, which consists of comprehensive inspections and repairs, being carried out on a DC-8. The aircraft's cockpit and passenger cabin were completely stripped down for this procedure. *SAS Museum*

The engine pod cross section has been reduced, and ducts carry fan air the entire length of the nacelle—thereby reducing drag losses. The improved pod is positioned 40 inches farther forward than the standard pod, for less interference between engine pod and wing.

Main landing-gear bogie beam
A new, simplified, single bogie beam that does not swivel is incorporated in each main landing gear to effect a weight saving of over 200 pounds over the basic DC-8 models. The new bogie beams are interchangeable, reducing maintenance and spare-parts requirements.

Repositioned flap and vane
All Series 60 model incorporate repositioned double-slotted flaps and vanes. The modification in relative position of flaps, vane, and wing in the flap-down position reduces drag and provides increased lift for takeoff and landing.

Hytrol braking and spoiler actuation
Mk. II Hytrol antiskid brakes are standard equipment on all Series 60 airplanes. Thy provide modulated pressure and maximum braking under all weather conditions. Spoiler actuation occurs on spin-up of main landing-gear wheels. This combination reduces landing rollout appreciably.

(*Source*: Douglas Aircraft Division brochure *The Douglas DC-8 Super 60s and DC-9 Series Airplanes*, printed in December 1965)

SPECIFICATIONS FOR THE SAS DC-8 FLEET

Because of the plethora of variants and subvariants of the different models of the DC-8, it is almost impossible to produce a database that is valid for several airlines. We would therefore like to take this opportunity to present the fleet of the Scandinavian airline SAS as representative of all other airlines. It also has subvariants, as described above, but at least it gives an indication of the technical specifications of its DC-8s. As a member of the KSSU Group, the SAS DC-8s were of the same technical standard as the DC-8s operated by KLM, Swissair, and UTA.

WARTUNG

Jede SAS Maschine wird von erfahrenen Spezialisten mit Hilfe modernster Prüfgeräte ständigen Kontrollen, in der Fachsprache »Checks« genannt, unterzogen: Vor dem Start, während des Fluges und bei anderen regelmäßigen Inspektionen.

Neben routinemäßigen Überprüfungen werden unsere Flugzeuge nach festgesetzten Zeiten regelmäßig zu Wartungsdiensten und kompletten Überholungen aus dem Verkehr gezogen.
Die periodischen Überholungen erfolgen in Kopenhagen, während die SAS-Werft in Oslo für Wartungen der Zelle von DC-9 und Metropolitan Maschinen zuständig ist. DC-8 und Caravelle Maschinen werden in der Arlanda-Werft in Stockholm überholt. Die Stockholmer Linta-Werft ist auf die Überholung der Düsentriebwerke spezialisiert. Als erste Fluglinie der Welt führte SAS das T.R.A.C.E (Tape Recorded Automatic Checkout Equipment) ein, ein automatisches Untersuchungsverfahren für Flugzeuge auf der Grundlage elektronischer Datenverarbeitung. Mit Hilfe dieses hochmodernen Gerätes können in Sekundenschnelle selbst winzigste Fehler entdeckt und durch Reparatur oder Austausch beseitigt werden. Wertvolle Arbeitszeit wird dadurch eingespart.

10

The maintaining of the airline's DC-8s was the focus of this advertisement from SAS. *SAS / author's collection*

DC-8-33

Engines: 4 Pratt & Whitney JT4-A9
Wingspan: 43.4 m (142 ft., 4 in.)
Length: 45.9 m (150 ft., 7 in.)
Maximum takeoff weight: 142,900 kg (315,040 lbs.)
Fuel capacity: 83,000 L (21,926 US gal.)
Maximum payload: 19,000 kg (41,888 lbs.)
Maximum speed: 950 kph (590 mph)
Cruising speed: 870 kph (540 mph)
Range: 6,500 km (4,039 mi.)
Passenger seats (first/economy class): 138
Cruise altitude: 10,000 m (33,000 ft.)
Cargo volume: 38.7 m^3 (1,366 ft.^{3})

DC-8-55

Engines: 4 Pratt & Whitney JT3D-3B
Wingspan: 43.4 m (142 ft., 4 in.)
Length: 45.9 m (150 ft., 7 in.)

Maximum takeoff weight: 147,400 kg (324,961 lbs.)
Fuel capacity: 90,000 l (23,775 US gal.)
Maximum speed: 950 kph (590 mph)
Cruising speed: 870 kph (540 mph)
Range: 8,400 km (6,219 mi.)
Passenger seats (first / economy class): 145
Cruise altitude: 10,000 m (33,000 ft.)
Cargo volume: 38.7 m^3 (1,366 $ft.^3$)

DC-8-62

Engines: 4 Pratt & Whitney JT3D-3B
Wingspan: 47.9 m (157 ft., 1.8 in.)
Length: 45.9 m (150 ft., 7 in.)
Maximum takeoff weight: 152,000 kg (335,102 lbs.)
Fuel capacity: 92,000 L (24,304 US gal.)
Maximum payload: 22,500 kg (49,604 lbs.)
Maximum speed: 950 kph (590 mph)
Cruising speed: 870 kph (540 mph)
Range: 9,800 km (6,089 mi.)
Passenger seats (first/economy class): 154
Cruise altitude: 10,000 m (33,000 ft.)
Cargo volume: 44 m^3 (1,554 $ft.^3$)

DC-8-62CF (PASSENGER/FREIGHT COMBI)

Engines: 4 Pratt & Whitney JT3D-3B
Wingspan: 45.2 m (148 ft., 3 in.)
Length: 47.9 m (157 ft., 1.8 in.)
Maximum takeoff weight: 152,000 kg (335,102 lbs.)
Fuel capacity: 92,000 L (24,304 US gal.)
Maximum payload: 22,500 kg (49,604 lbs.)
Maximum speed: 950 kph (590 mph)
Cruising speed: 870 kph (540 mph)
Range: 9,800 km (6,089 mi.)
Passenger seats (first/economy class): 154
Cruise altitude: 10,000 m (33,000 ft.)
Cargo volume: 44.8 m^3 (1,582 $ft.^3$)

DC-8-62AF (FREIGHT ONLY)

Engines: 4 Pratt & Whitney JT3D-3B
Wingspan: 45.2 m (148 ft., 3 in.)
Length: 47.9 m (157 ft., 1.8 in.)
Maximum takeoff weight: 152,000 kg (335,102 lbs.)
Cargo compartment volume: 209.7 m^3 (7,405 $ft.^3$)
Fuel capacity: 92,000 L (24,304 US gal.)
Maximum payload: 22,500 kg (49,604 lbs.)
Maximum speed: 950 kph (590 mph)
Cruising speed: 870 kph (540 mph)
Range: 9,800 km (6,089 mi.)
Passenger seats (first/economy class): 154
Cruise altitude: 10,000 m (33,000 ft.)
Cargo volume: 44.8 m^3 (1,582 $ft.^3$)

DC-8-63

Engines: 4 Pratt & Whitney JT3D-7
Wingspan: 45.2 m (148 ft., 3 in.)
Length: 57.1 m (187 ft., 4 in.)
Maximum takeoff weight: 161,000 kg (354,944 lbs.)
Fuel capacity: 92,000 L (24,304 US gal.)
Maximum payload: 30,300 kg (66,800 lbs.)
Maximum speed: 950 kph (590 mph)
Cruising speed: 870 kph (540 mph)
Range: 8,300 km (5,157 mi.)
Passenger seats (first/economy class): 194
Cruise altitude: 10,000 m (33,000 ft.)
Cargo volume: 70 m^3 (2,472 $ft.^3$)

CHAPTER 10
COMPETITION

Pan Am was the first customer for both the DC-8 and the Boeing 707. Although it initially ordered five fewer examples of the Boeing jet in 1955, the 707 was to become its preferred four-engine jet. The DC-8 lost out. *Boeing*

BOEING 707

BOEING 707-80 DASH 80

Wingspan: 39.6 m (129 ft., 11 in.)
Length: 39.01 m (127 ft., 11 in.)
Height: 11.6 m (38 ft.)
Engines: 4 Pratt & Whitney J-57
Cruise speed: 885 kph (550 mph)
Range: 3,700 km (2,299 mi.)
Cruise altitude: 12,800 m (41,995 ft.)
Cockpit crew: 3

BOEING 707-120

Wingspan: 39.88 m (130 ft., 10 in.)
Length: 44.22 m (145 ft., 1 in.)
Height: 12.70 m (41 ft., 8 in.)
Engines: 4 Pratt & Whitney JT3C (JT3D)
Max. takeoff weight, B version: 117,000 kg
Max. fuel load: 65,590 L (17,327 US gal.)
Max. seating capacity: 174
Cockpit crew: 4, including navigator on long-range flights

BOEING 707-420

Wingspan: 43.40 m (142 ft., 5 in.)
Length: 46.61 m (152 ft., 9 in.)
Height: 12.72 m (41 ft., 9 in.)
Engines: 4 Rolls-Royce Conway turbofans
Max. takeoff weight: 141,700 kg (312,395 lbs.)
Max. fuel load: 90,160 L (23,817 US gal.)
Max. seating capacity: 189
Cockpit crew: 4, including navigator on long-range flights

BOEING 707-320

Wingspan: 43.40 m (142 ft., 5 in.)
Length: 46.61 m (152 ft., 9 in.)
Height: 12.85 m (42 ft., 2 in.)
Engines: 4 Pratt & Whitney JT4A
Max. takeoff weight: 141,700 kg (312,395 lbs.)
Max. fuel load: 90,160 L (23,817 US gal.)
Max. seating capacity: 189
Cockpit crew: 3

BOEING 707-320B

Wingspan: 44.42 m (145 ft., 9 in.)
Length: 46.61 m (152 ft., 9 in.)
Height: 2.83 m (42 ft., 1 in.)
Engines: 4 Pratt & Whitney JT3D
Max. takeoff weight: 148,500 (151,500 kg)
Max. fuel load: 90,290 L (23,852 US gal.)
Max. seating capacity: 189
Cockpit crew: 3

BOEING 707-320C

Wingspan: 44.42 m (145 ft., 9 in.)
Length: 46.61 m (152 ft., 9 in.)
Height: 12.80 m (41 ft., 11.9 in.)
Engines: 4 Pratt & Whitney JT3D
Max. takeoff weight: 151,500 kg (334,000 lbs.)
Max. fuel load: 90,290 L (23,852 US gal.)
Max. seating capacity: 194 (combi version)
Cockpit crew: 3

BOEING 720

Wingspan: 39.88 m (130 ft., 10 in.)
Length: 41.30 m (135 ft., 6 in.)
Height: 12.62 m (41 ft., 5 in.)
Engines: 4 Pratt & Whitney JT3C
Max. takeoff weight: 104,000 kg (229,280 lbs.)
Max. fuel load: 60,900 L (16,088 US gal.)
Max. seating capacity: 149*
Cockpit crew: 3

* Optional 156 with installation of two additional type III emergency exits over the wings

BOEING 720B

Wingspan: 39.88 m (130 ft., 10 in.)
Length: 41.68m (136 ft., 9 in.)
Height: 12.55 m (41 ft., 2 in.)
Engines: 4 Pratt & Whitney JT3D
Max. takeoff weight: 106,200 kg (234,130 lbs.)
Max. fuel load: 61,300 L (16,194 US gal.)

Max. seating capacity: 149*
Cockpit crew: 3

* Optional 156 with installation of two additional type III emergency exits over the wings

Source: Boeing

For a long time, Boeing kept a big secret about the jet that was finally presented to the world at its ceremonial rollout on May 14, 1954. Two years earlier, the Boeing Board of Directors had given the go-ahead for the construction of the 367-80 test aircraft, whose name was intended to give the misleading impression that the Dash 80 was merely a further development of the Boeing 367 Stratofreighter military propeller-driven aircraft of the 1940s. Initial preliminary designs were strongly reminiscent of the company's own B-47 bomber or the Type 152 developed by Baade in Dresden, Germany, but after detailed investigations, Boeing engineers quickly rejected the concept of a high-wing aircraft for the planned new passenger jet. The arrangement of the systems and landing gear seemed too complex. What emerged as an alternative on the drawing boards of the Boeing design department until it was ready for production was a technological sensation at the time and, from today's perspective, nothing less than the beginning of modern civil jet aircraft construction. With the low-wing design chosen for the Dash 80, for example, the flight control cables and supply lines could be arranged between the cabin floor and the cargo hold below to save space, which would not have been possible with a high-wing layout. After about thirty studies, which were tested for their practical suitability in Boeing's own high-speed wind tunnel, the Dash 80 design crystallized, and even the then-seventy-two-year-old company founder, William Boeing, took part in its rollout. His wife, Bertha, christened the airplane with a bottle of "real champagne," as the Boeing chronicle notes. Just how advanced the Dash 80 was sixty-five years ago can be seen in its basic design, which still lives on today in Boeing's best-selling 737 and has become firmly established in the public eye as the epitome of a modern airliner. However, numerous Boeing jets have their roots not only visually but also technologically in this pioneering test aircraft of the early 1950s. Its wings swept back by 35 degrees, the engines mounted on pylons under the wings, and the basic layout of its systems made the Dash 80 the design ancestor of the Boeing 717 (KC-135), 707, and 720. However, various design features can also be found in the 727, 737, and 757 aircraft families to this day. The design of this Boeing jet prototype was so striking that even on a modern airport apron, most observers would hardly recognize the Dash 80 as a sixty-five-year-old jet.

Boeing used its 367-80 as a research aircraft to gather important data for the design of passenger aircraft, but also as a demonstration aircraft for potential customers. Not only managers but also pilots and engineers from the world's leading airlines gathered in Seattle. Among them was the charismatic Pan American founder and president Juan T. Trippe, who was looking for a suitable aircraft type for his company's entry into the jet age on long-haul routes.

The first public presentation was followed by the much-noticed maiden flight of the Dash 80 on July 15, 1954. Although the experts were enthusiastic, the airlines were reluctant to place firm orders for the 707 jetliner, which had been developed from the 367-80. This was mainly because Boeing was offering its first four-engine jet with a small fuselage cross section—in which the airlines showed no interest. In contrast to the competing Douglas DC-8, whose wide fuselage comfortably accommodated six-abreast seating, Boeing offered its 707 with a narrower fuselage cross section and a maximum of five-abreast seating. The engineers had already widened the cross section to 12 feet (3.66 m) compared to the Dash 80, but this was still not enough for the airlines. The 717/707 program threatened to end in a financial fiasco for Boeing until the US Department of Defense came to the rescue and initially ordered twenty-one Boeing 717 (KC-135) tanker aircraft in February 1955, which would later result in orders for 808 aircraft! At the time, the KC-135 had the same fuselage width as the civil 707, which enabled Boeing to plan and finance both projects at the same time, thanks to this military order. Even when Pan American president Trippe ordered twenty

707s as the launch customer on October 13, 1955, there was little reason for Boeing to celebrate—the charismatic airline boss announced in the same breath that this was his airline's first and last order for the new Boeing jet, and that the DC-8, of which Pan Am ordered twenty-five at the same time, was clearly favored thanks to its wider fuselage.

The fact that the 707 cabin cross section was then widened by 3.9 inches (10 cm) to 12.3 feet (3.76 m)—which also made it possible to install six seats per row—was due to the persistence of American Airlines. Its management was able to persuade Boeing to change its mind and rewarded the aircraft manufacturer's insight with an order for thirty aircraft placed on November 8, 1955. Not only was the 707 now available on the market a year earlier than the DC-8, but its cabin dimensions were even a few centimeters larger than those of its Californian competitor. The race for orders was on, and in the end, Boeing was the clear winner. While Douglas sold 556 civil versions of the DC-8, Boeing sold 754 Boeing 707s and 154 Boeing 720s. Including military variants, Boeing produced a total of 1,010 Boeing 707s and 808 of the 717 (KC-135) tanker. The pioneering spirit shown by then Boeing president Bill Allen in the 1950s paid off in hard cash for the company and made Seattle one of the centers of civil aircraft construction in the Western world.

JETS CONQUER THE NORTH ATLANTIC

Three years after its spectacular order placed with Boeing and Douglas, Pan Am was able to take off into the jet age over the North Atlantic—twenty-two days after the British airline BOAC, which had won the race for the first scheduled transatlantic flight by a jet airliner with the completely redesigned Comet 4. It was a late success for de Havilland, but not one that could give the Comet program a decisive boost. It was discontinued in 1964 after twelve years of production and 113 aircraft delivered.

On October 26, 1958, Pan Am's Boeing 707-121, christened Jet Clipper America and bearing the registration N711PA, took off from New York for the first commercial flight of this type, bound for Paris. In addition to the smooth, fast flight above the clouds, passengers on the Pan Am jet service were able to enjoy another innovation for the first time: economy class. Compared to the tourist class introduced on propeller-driven airliners in 1952, Economy was around 20 percent cheaper. Compared to the offerings of most airlines in 2019, the seat spacing between rows was still extremely generous, and the service on board was opulent. The Boeing 707 thus made a significant contribution to making air travel accessible to a wider audience, which meant that the aircraft slowly began to lose its original nimbus as an exclusive means of transportation for the "rich and beautiful." In 1959, a Pan Am first-class ticket cost 783 US dollars for a return flight between New York and London. The same journey in economy class was offered on the Boeing 707 for 436 US dollars, which is equivalent to 940 Euros today due to the much-higher value of the US dollar at the time. The relatively low fares and short flight times made the new long-haul jet a popular alternative to competing ocean liners, and 1962 was the first year in which more passengers flew across the North Atlantic than sailed on passenger ships. In the first three months of 1959, Pan Am carried 33,400 paying passengers on its Boeing 707 fleet—almost unrivaled in its first year of operation. Apart from BOAC's smaller Comet 4, which often had to make refueling stops between the Old World and the New, there were no other jets flying on scheduled North Atlantic routes. The reason: Pan Am had blocked the Boeing 707 final-assembly line for almost twelve months with its orders, and the Douglas DC-8-32, the only serious competitor, would not become available until 1960.

THE 707 JET INTERCONTINENTAL

The initial order for the Boeing 707-120 by Pan American World Airways was preceded by an unprecedented game of poker between the airline, on the one hand, and aircraft manufacturers Boeing and Douglas, on the other hand. Lockheed president Gross, who was also invited to submit a bid, had refused to participate in the Pan Am tender on the grounds that two comparable aircraft types would be sufficient for the expected demand. Juan Trippe, who had founded the world's most prestigious airline on October 28, 1928, at the age of twenty-eight, was initially the only airline boss to show any interest in the four-engine designs from Boeing and Douglas. This gave him all the trump cards—and he knew how to use them. Above all, the fate of the civil Boeing 707 project depended on his order. He initially launched the 707-120, which still had a relatively short range and allowed nonstop flights across the North Atlantic only under favorable weather conditions. However, the Pan Am president had specific ideas about what his ideal long-haul jet should look like. Douglas was the first manufacturer willing to develop its basic DC-8 model to Pan Am's requirements around the then-new and more powerful Pratt & Whitney J-75 engine (the later JT4), resulting in the DC-8-32 long-range version. If they did not want to lose the lucrative order completely to their Californian competitor, the aircraft manufacturers from Seattle also had to improve their basic model. After long, tough negotiations, Boeing president Bill Allen finally agreed to supplement the Boeing 707-120, powered by the Pratt & Whitney JT3 engine, with a new version with a greater wingspan, a longer fuselage, greater range, and the more powerful JT4 engine—and the Boeing 707-320 Intercontinental was born. Thanks to the perseverance of Juan Trippe, the most successful of all Boeing 707 variants was created, and it succeeded in winning a large number of orders, especially as the B model, powered by JT3D engines.

Pan Am was also so enthusiastic about its 707 jets that, contrary to the original announcement in 1955, it took delivery of only nineteen of the twenty-five DC-8-32s originally ordered from Douglas and instead operated not just twenty, but ultimately 128 Boeing 707s and nine Boeing 720Bs over the years!

The CV 880 was Convair's momentous attempt to establish itself as the third manufacturer of four-engine passenger jets. However, the joint CV 880 and CV 990 projects led to the aircraft manufacturer narrowly avoiding bankruptcy. The CV 880 was too small, while the CV 990 failed to meet expectations in terms of speed and range. *Jon Proctor*

CONVAIR CV 880

CV 880 GOLDEN ARROW

Manufacturer: General Dynamics/Convair, San Diego, California
Maiden flight: January 27, 1959
Number built: 65
Wingspan: 36.58 m (120 ft.)
Length: 39.42 m (129 ft., 4 in.)
Height: 11.00 m (36 ft.)
Engines: 4 General Electric CJ-805-3
Cruise speed: approx. 990 kph (615 mph)
Range: approx. 4,400 km (2,734 mi.)
Crew: 3 on the flight deck

The Consolidated Vultee Aircraft Corporation, or Convair for short, was a well-known name among the traveling public, especially in Europe. Their very comfortably equipped Metropolitans were flown in the 1950s and 1960s by Iberia, Finnair, Lufthansa, SAS, and Swissair, among others, and were synonymous with relaxed flying in the golden age of air travel. In contrast to the two major American manufacturers of passenger jets, Boeing and Douglas, Convair had excellent contacts with one of the most colorful figures in American aviation in the mid-1950s: Howard Hughes. As the first billionaire in US history, oil magnate, film producer, and aviation entrepreneur, he asked Convair management whether they could develop and manufacture a jet with transcontinental range for Trans World Airlines (TWA), which he controlled. Had Convair management realized at this point that Howard Hughes's airs and graces would lead not only to orders, but also to the impending ruin of the Convair aircraft factories, the CV 880 might never have been produced in the first place.

THE GOLDEN ARROW

After numerous design studies, Convair presented the final draft of the jetliner, powered by four General Electric CJ-805 engines and named Skylark 600, in 1956 in the hope of winning a large slice of the civil jet market. On June 7, 1956, the Tool Company (Toolco), part of the Hughes empire, through which Hughes acquired all TWA aircraft and leased them to the airline, signed preliminary contracts with Convair and General Electric for thirty examples of the jetliner, now named the Golden Arrow. Delta Air Lines followed on the same day with an order for ten aircraft, although Toolco, as the larger customer, was free to determine the delivery date.

Convair got its first taste of Howard Hughes's eccentric ideas when he requested that the aircraft be made of shimmering golden metal. However, the jet, now called the Golden Arrow, remained an idée fixe, since there was no manufacturing process at the time that guaranteed a uniform golden color for all fuselage and wing panels.

When the two initial customers, Toolco (TWA) and Delta Air Lines, converted their purchase options into firm orders for a total of forty aircraft on September 10, 1956, there was no more talk of the Golden Arrow. Instead, the aircraft project was now given its final name, the Convair 880. With a cruising speed of almost 1,000 kilometers per hour (621 mph), the 880 is still one of the fastest passenger aircraft today.

After these initial interventions in the aircraft program, Convair was to experience what it meant to do business with Howard Hughes, especially during the production phase. Production of the first aircraft had made good progress at the Convair plant in San Diego, and nothing stood in the way of the contractually agreed delivery of the jets to TWA and Delta between fall 1959 and September 1960, when a team of Toolco inspectors appeared unannounced on the final-assembly line in July 1959. The first two CV 880s destined for TWA, which were due for delivery in November and December 1959, aroused their particular interest. This happened without the knowledge of the TWA management, who found out about the events only through their own team on-site! The situation came to a dramatic head in an almost surreal way when the team of inspectors arrived in October of that year, accompanied by armed guards who locked down both aircraft. No Convair or TWA employees were allowed to approach the aircraft, let alone enter them. There was certainly no question of continuing their final assembly. As it turned out, a few days after the siege of the Convair production hall by the Toolco guards, Howard Hughes had issued this order personally. With difficulty, Convair managed to keep the final-assembly line running and was thus able to deliver at least the first CV 880 to Delta Air Lines on February 9, 1960.

However, the drama surrounding the aircraft destined for Toolco dragged on throughout 1960. Hughes categorically refused to accept the 880 fleet destined for TWA, but he refused to offer a reason.

It seems like an act of desperation that TWA bought one of the aircraft ordered by Toolco with its own money in May 1960 so as to at least use this CV 880 as a crew trainer for the hoped-for entry into service of the remaining twenty-nine aircraft.

The situation eased for TWA only on December 30, 1960, after Howard Hughes lost control of the airline because of financial problems. On the same day, Toolco transferred the delivery positions for nineteen CV 880s to TWA, the first of which was handed over to the airline just two days later. By January 18, 1961, the fleet had grown to five, including the training aircraft acquired in May 1960. Freed from the hindrances of Howard Hughes, Convair set about quickly completing the remaining jets that had been "trapped" on the final-assembly line.

TWA began scheduled service with its new Convair airliners on January 12, 1961. The new flagship of the TWA fleet then began setting one speed record after another; for example, on January 24, 1961, on the route from Chicago to New York. At an average speed of 1,094 kilometers per hour (670.8 mph), the flight time was just one hour and eleven minutes. The Convairs, christened the StarStream 880 by TWA, were initially equipped with eighty-five first-class and only twenty-nine coach-class seats. In the forward cabin area, a first-class lounge with twelve armchairs also invited passengers to enjoy a drink above the clouds.

In addition to its extremely luxurious seating, the CV 880 impressed with its sophisticated cabin design. Harley Earl, chief designer at General Motors and "father of the GM Corvette," was commissioned by Convair to design a passenger cabin that would counteract the oppressive tube effect from the perspective of passengers in the rear rows of seats. His solution: He lowered the cabin roof by a few centimeters every five rows of seats, thus creating a visual division into smaller segments.

Despite all its progressive ideas, Convair's CV 880 was not a success. This was due in no small part to Howard Hughes, whose reckless behavior threw the CV 880 final-assembly line into chaos and did not allow Convair to use their completed aircraft for demonstration flights to potential customers. Thus, deprived of the opportunity to market its jet successfully, Convair produced only sixty-five examples of the basic CV 880 and the further developed CV 880M at a loss. Nevertheless, the CV 880 deserves its place among the legendary jetliners, since its design was so attractive that several renowned airlines around the globe placed orders. These included Cathay Pacific, Civil Air Transport, and Japan Air Lines in Asia, as well as the Venezuelan airline VIASA in Latin America. In the USA, customers for brand-new aircraft included Delta, TWA, Alaska Airlines, and Northeast. CV 880s also flew in the colors of KLM and Swissair in Europe. The latter used the Convair jets as a temporary solution until the larger CV 990 was delivered. Lisa Marie—Elvis Presley's private CV 880—became world famous. Today, it can be seen in the Memphis Rock 'n' Soul Museum in Tennessee.

VICKERS VC10

Manufacturer: Vickers-Armstrongs Aircraft Ltd., Weybridge, Great Britain
Maiden flight: June 29, 1962
Number built: 54
Wingspan: 44.55 m (146 ft., 2 in.)
Length: 48.36 m (158 ft., 8 in.)
Height: 12.04 m (39 ft., 6 in.)
Engines: 4 Rolls-Royce Conway 540 turbofans
Cruise speed: approx. 900 kph (559 mph)
Range: approx. 8,000 km (4,970 mi.)
Crew: 3–4 on the flight deck
(specification, Standard VC-10 version)

The Vickers VC10 was undoubtedly an extremely elegant aircraft. However, it was equally unsuccessful. The reason: Vickers had to design the aircraft with a performance solely intended for BOAC's (now British Airways) African route network. This made the airliner of little interest to most other airlines around the world. *Vickers / author's collection*

The Vickers VC10 was the result of a tender issued by the British state airline BOAC, which needed a modern long-haul jet-powered aircraft for its routes to the Far East and Africa. The new jetliner had to be capable of flying nonstop to England with a full payload, even from the short runways of the airports in the BOAC route network that were located in subtropical regions. At the request of the British government, the Vickers Aircraft Company, based in Brooklands near London, therefore developed a completely new aircraft that was specifically tailored to BOAC's requirements.

A LITTLE VC10DERNESS

In January 1958 the airline finally placed an order for thirty-five aircraft, with options on another twenty. This was followed two years later by an order for the larger Super VC10, whose fuselage was stretched by more than 2 m compared to the standard version. But even before the first aircraft was delivered, BOAC management realized that the now-six-year-old operational plan for the VC10 was obsolete. The runways at the British Commonwealth's African and Asian airports had been expanded in the meantime, which made it possible to use other, more-economical models. BOAC therefore urged that the thirty Super VC10s ordered be canceled. After long negotiations among the airline, Vickers, and the British government, BOAC was allowed to reduce the order to twelve Standard and seventeen Super VC10s.

The two VC10 variants, which entered service in 1964 and 1965, impressed with their elegance and were very popular with passengers. Due to their large wings, whose aerodynamics were not disturbed by engine nacelles, as was the case with other jet airliners, the VC10s flew extremely quietly. The same was true of the cabin, which because of the four rear-mounted engines was little affected by the noise they produced. BOAC used the advertising slogan "A Little VC10derness" to emphasize the outstanding passenger comfort on board the elegant aircraft.

In addition to BOAC and British United Airways (BUA), the four-engine aircraft flew with various airlines in the Middle East and on the African continent. Some Standard VC10s were also used as VIP jets in the Gulf region. Until the fall of 2013, the British Royal Air Force used a number of Vickers VC10s as troop transports and for aerial refueling of military jets.

The fact that this type was not a sales success can be attributed to the fact that it was tailored too specifically to BOAC's original requirements. The VC10 was tailor-made for an airline that would have preferred not to put this jet into service at all.

The days until the very last takeoff by a DC-8 were numbered when this book was written. *Dirk Grothe*

BIBLIOGRAPHY

Contemporaneous documents, Douglas.

Contemporaneous documents, Pan Am.

Contemporaneous documents, SAS.

Contemporaneous documents, Swissair.

Contemporaneous documents, United.

Roach, J. R., and A. B. Eastwood. *Jet Airliner Production List, 1949–1989.*

ACKNOWLEDGMENTS

Numerous people and organizations contributed to the success of this book. I would like to thank, in particular, Marcus Kolskog, of Sweden, who provided me with his entire DC-8 collection for this book; Dirk Grothe, of Germany, who provided his own DC-8 photos for this book; and Tom Weihe and Nicolai Larsen Musante, of Denmark. Tom provided his own historical DC-8 photographs, which Nicolai put the finishing touches on for publication in this book. I thank as well my beloved wife, Carol Oxberry, with her continued support of advice and patience in the creation of this book!

THE AUTHOR

Wolfgang Borgmann's enthusiasm for aviation was passed on to him by his parents, who were active in the aviation field. In his early years, he began building up an aviation historical collection that provides numerous rare photos and documents, as well as exciting background information, for his books. Since April 2000, Borgmann has been active as an author and freelance aviation journalist. He lives in Bielefeld, Germany.

His website is www.aerojournalist.de.